Breakthrough into Deeper Intimacy with God

Rory MaGrath

Experience God's presence in your life
in a real and fulfilling way

malcolm down
PUBLISHING

British Library Cataloguing in Publication Data
A catalogue record for this book is available from the British Library.

ISBN: 978-1-915046-69-7

Cover design by Esther Kotecha
Art direction by Sarah Grace

Printed in the UK

About the Author

Rory was born in 1972 in Port Elizabeth, Eastern Cape, South Africa, and grew up in the province of Kwa-Zulu Natal, in a town called Ladysmith. His father was an Assemblies of God pastor (currently retired) in various South African towns.

Rory was involved in the SCA (Students' Christian Association) at school and was made chairman of the SCA in his final year. He then went on to do courses in both Homiletics and Hermeneutics within the church. After completing his military conscription in the South African Defence Force's Engineering Corps, he studied for three years as a Medical Tech., then after six years switched careers and went into construction. In 2010, he completed a certificate in Bible Theology through SATS (South African Theological Seminary).

Rory married his wife Pauline in May 2009, and they moved to the UK in October 2016. They now reside in Leeds, West Yorkshire, where Rory is actively involved in their local church. He works full-time as a Construction Project Manager, whilst in his free time he works to help people overcome various dependencies and guides others to establishing a real relationship with God, as well as continuing to write.

From 1990 to 2006, Rory drifted away from the Lord, and for seventeen years his life changed to one of "living hell". The road back was painful and long but, through it, he experienced an amazing miracle that brought him into the close and personal relationship that he has with God today. Rory's first book, *Breakthrough into Recovery*, was published in the UK in July 2018 (previously in SA in 2015). He has been involved with, and supported, many recovery institutions and has started a few Christian support groups in various churches. With it has come an overwhelming desire to help people experience a deeper, more heart-felt closeness with God.

The author can be contacted at: btilrbgod@gmail.com

This book is dedicated to my father and mother
(Mike and Heather), for their unceasing love
and prayer for me; I love you both.

*"The effectual fervent prayer of a
righteous man availeth much."*

(James 5:16b)

Acknowledgements

Firstly, I want to thank my Father God through Jesus Christ for what He has done in my life. If I hadn't been an alcoholic, I would not have come to the point of desperation where I was truly willing to seek Him; I was just that stubborn and self-centred. I want to thank Him for the pain and hardship He gracefully granted me. I now know that while I went through "living hell", He was looking after me the whole time. Ego makes you feel consciously separated from God, and I believe this must be a bit of what hell is like. If it were not for this experience, I would not have the wonderful relationship I have with Him today. Because of His love, mercy and grace, I am living a life of peace, joy and contentment.

Secondly, I would like to thank the organisation of Alcoholics Anonymous for showing me a workable solution that led me to God, who is the ultimate source of all power. I would also like to thank all those in the meetings that showed me unconditional love; to have a group of strangers love you "warts 'n' all" with no hidden agenda other than to see you recover, was truly a unique experience.

Next, I'd like to thank my mother and father for their love and prayers. I know it was not easy at times, especially when there was nothing you could do but let go and pray. I am grateful for your unceasing intercession, that you were able to entrust me to God, and that you never lost hope. I feel that God honoured you by setting me free and moving into relationship with me.

I would also like to thank my wife Pauline, who has been a support to me for many years now. Although I had been relieved of alcoholism before we met, I know it has not always been easy, and yet you remained loving and supportive. God has truly blessed you with the unfading beauty of a gentle and quiet spirit. Your loving support has allowed me to grow in the Lord, and I love you very much.

Thank you to Karin, Alan and Anne for sharing your life-changing stories so openly with us; may God continue to grow and deepen your relationships with Him, as He uses you to touch the lives of those seeking Him.

Finally, I would like to thank the various Spirit-filled authors and speakers that God has used to shape and mould my Christian walk and belief; I have grown immensely through this. For this book, I would like to give special thanks to the late pastor Andrew Murray. His book *Humility* had really helped me to strengthen the foundations in my Christianity, and it was a strong influence in the writing of my first book. However, it was during the writing of this book that God used the late pastor Andrew's book *Absolute Surrender* to give real revelation to what it meant to be a Christian, and what it took to be in deep and intimate relationship with God. Thanks to the strength of this revelation, I am now convinced that I need to trust God for absolutely everything, and that only He can give me the power to *will*, and then to *do*.

Contents

Introduction

I am writing this book three years after my first book (*Breakthrough into Recovery*), as I have come to realize in my daily living that this solution, which helped me recover from alcoholism, is something that has drawn me into an almost *tangible* relationship with God, the depth of which I never thought possible.

If you have truthfully had thoughts of why so many Christian people talk about these marvellous experiences and truly close relationships they have with God, yet wondered why you are not experiencing this realism in your own relationship with God, then this book is for you. During my life I had often asked myself this type of question. From as soon as I was old enough to understand God, and to ponder what I was supposed to "do" with God, and how I was supposed to feel and interact with Him, I had asked this question.

I never felt God the same way others saw or described Him, and I was not going to let on that I never experienced anything they were describing. I never really experienced God at all, to be truthful; He seemed to be there but not involved with me. I prayed for Him to make Himself real to me on many occasions over the first thirty-three years of my life, but nothing changed. I had enough conviction to believe in His existence and the fact that Jesus had paid the penance for my sin, but that was where it ended. I had more fear of going to hell than worrying about a relationship with God, and this is why I went through the motions of church and pretended that things were real and godly for me.

When my first book was published in the UK, a lot of my friends and family read it even though they did not suffer from any dependency disorders, and I started noticing a pattern on their feedback. There were quite a few of them who have said that they have been challenged into a new way of looking at their relationship with God. Although there are only a few who have read the book that do not have any dependency disorders, I would say that more than 60 per cent of them have said that their relationship with God has changed since they started implementing the solution offered in this book to their lives.

This did not surprise me as I had quickly come to realize during my own recovery that alcohol had not been my problem, but rather my solution that had stopped working, and that the true problem I had had nothing to do with alcohol at all. I realized that many others were dealing with the same truths I had faced from a young child, and that the truth was that we never felt we had a *real* connection or relationship with God, but rather that we were false; pretending and mimicking what we heard and saw others doing.

I was surprised at how easily it seemed to work in others when I compared it to working with people that had addictions. At this point I was reminded that as an alcoholic, I had been an extreme case of self-will run riot. We had often been told this in the group meetings, but it seems it took a while for the dynamics of this statement to make sense to me. The level of pain and desperation that was needed for me to be willing to follow the process, was not necessarily needed for those who were feeling an emptiness or a lack of real intimacy with God. It was then that I started getting promptings from the Lord to write another book that would incorporate a similar process, but one which would apply to the everyday person or churchgoer who may feel they are missing something in their lives or in their connection with God.

The solution proffered in the book is nothing more than a spiritual set of tools laid out in a step-for-step guide, explained through my experiences and a few suggestions that have worked during my own journey in bringing me into the incredible relationship with God that I have today. For me, I had to have something I could follow and actually *work* at. For too long there were only suggestions of what I was supposed to do to achieve something, and not a whole lot about *how* to do it.

I have shared a lot of my experiences, and I talk a lot about the process, steps and programme in this book, but I do want to be clear that I can only truly share *my* experiences with conviction, as I have not lived anyone else's. In doing so, I am trusting that the Holy Spirit will help you to relate or identify with something I have shared. The process, steps or Program are only a method, guide or spiritual set of tools to help us connect with God, through His Son Jesus, by the power of the Holy Spirit. I trust that in my writing you see that humility is the key to God lifting us up (James 4:10).

The awareness of my powerlessness has ended up being my greatest asset. I believe this has come about through the revelation of the Holy Spirit, and this only after I diligently went through the process detailed in this book. This is something I will explain early on, and it is wonderfully liberating when you get your head around the fact that there is actually really little for us to do, and that the outcome and result will have nothing to do with us either. I was prompted mainly by pain and then desperation to work this Program. However, I believe that this level of pain is not needed for others if there is a sincere desire to have a deeper relationship with God. I am trusting that you will have picked up this book because you do not sense a real presence of God in your life, or maybe because there is a feeling of something missing in your spiritual walk with God. I would suggest that you would have to be *truly* honest with yourself about how you really experience God in your own personal walk with Him. You will know deep-down inside yourself what the truth is. If you cannot be honest yet, that's ok, I wasn't either in the beginning. I would say a strong willingness and a semblance of open-mindedness would suffice. A willingness to actually start reading the book, and an open-mindedness to the fact that there may actually be a very simple, different approach and way of looking at things, one which may differ to the one you have grown up with. I am not sharing anything new or *far-out* in this solution, and you will be able to verify everything in the book by the standards set in the Word of God. I believe that the Bible is the plumb line against which all else in this world is measured. If it goes against the Word of God, I don't do it.

Over the last few years of observation and interaction with Christians, I have come to realize how few seem to really *know* Him on an intimate level, and I can totally relate to them. This was the big thing for me; I had the belief and trust in my salvation, but because I wasn't experiencing anything *real* in my dealings with God, I felt like a big "phony". I hated that feeling, but I was not going to tell anyone that this is what I felt, because that would be embarrassing. I felt restless, irritable and generally discontent with my lot in life – it all seemed a bit boring and empty.

This is why I have written this book, because I believe that anyone can quickly move into the heart-felt relationship with God that we may have heard others speak about. I'm talking about the kind of relationship that is so naturally real, that it appears almost tangible, like God is actually there in the room, or in the car with you.

For me to find myself in this level of relationship with our Lord required a process, with promptings and suggestions to follow. I am so privileged that this was shown to me, and that I was in a place of willingness to actually *do* what was suggested of me. I have laid down this process step for step, precisely as I did it, and I have included personal examples and worksheets. I wanted to make it easy to work through, because it was that simple for me – praise God!

The working parts of the book are full of personal examples I have included from my life, and you will find the web address where you can download and print off the necessary worksheet templates for free. There are personal worksheet examples in the book as well, so you can physically draw them up if you don't have access to a computer or printer at any time. It is really simple, like a cake recipe, and I have gone into as much detail as I could so as to eliminate as much doubt and confusion as possible. If you are not sure of something, I would suggest a quick prayer to the Lord, and then go with your gut-feel; it will all work out just fine. A gut-feel is often the prompting of the Holy Spirit, and even if we judge it wrong, God can work all things out for good (Romans 8:28). There are parts of the book where interaction with others will be necessary, but I believe that God's grace will be granted to the sincere reader so that a sufficient amount of fear will leave them at the appropriate time, allowing them to make the connection with the relevant people – it certainly worked that way for me.

You do not need to understand that much actually; you need to do the work. Reading the book might bring some understanding and relief, but it is only when you *do* the work that the miracle takes place, and that is biblical:

> *But wilt thou know, O vain man, that faith without works is dead?*
> James 2:20

I believe one of the main problems we all face in our lives comes from our fleshly nature, and that is *self*.[1] I believe that this *self* is what cuts us off from a real relationship with God. The dilemma I faced was that I could not really see this selfishness in myself, and this is why I believe I needed a process to follow; essentially a process of ego-deflation. I don't believe anyone can allow God to remove *self* until they can truly see they have it.

This is the process, in a nutshell. It is an absolutely incredible experience to go through, and to see how quickly and easily God's power flows through the situation.

---

1. Here "self" refers to selfishness, self-centeredness, self-focus, self-attention, self-obsession, self-absorption, etc.

Without me even realizing it initially, I had moved into this deep relationship with God. It was a mind-blowing experience for me, and I often wonder how I could have survived without this relationship I now have with Him. It was better than anything I could imagine, and God wants an intimate relationship with you too!

I would like to make a few suggestions and explanations so that you may get the most out of reading this book and doing the work needed for this vital connection to God's power. Before you read or do any work from this book each time, I suggest you pray a short one-line prayer. The power comes from God, and praying is our most direct communication with Him. Pray for strength, grace, understanding, peace and willingness.

I found an important part of going through the process was an attitude of willingness. In order for me to be this committed to anything, I had to be convinced that those presenting the spiritual set of tools to me (the ones telling me that their intimate relationship with God was found in this Program), had initially battled to form a real relationship with God just as I had. That is why I have put so much of my own personal experience into the book; I cannot give away what I don't have. I know this is not the only path to finding intimacy with God, but I have tried many others, and this is the only one that has worked for me. When reading these experiences, you are unlikely to find an exact match to your own situation but try to identify with as much as possible of what you read; try to relate mainly to the outlook and "feelings" described. As I had to recover from alcoholism, you will find that many of the experiences I had were to do with what the alcoholism brought on. I still think you will probably find that you can relate to quite a few of the stories, especially the feelings and thoughts involved. Once you make this connection, you should feel a sense of hope rise within you. I recommend that you continue to read the book in the sequence and format in which it is laid out. There might be a few misgivings that will rarely be dispelled properly until you start the *action* parts of the book. My suggestion is to try not to skip chapters or sections; this will give you a more solid foundation to work from.

In the book you will see that I have included a few real-life short stories written by others who have worked through the solution laid out in this book, and I pray that this may give you encouragement and hope that this Program really works in people who were in a similar situation to yourself.

You may notice that I may repeat certain things within the book, and this is no mistake – there are two main reasons for doing this. The first is that if there is something of high importance to learn or remember, I found that it sticks better through repetition; it is like a constant reminder, and it gets me to start thinking along these lines as second nature. I find that the Bible does this as well, and I cannot count the amount of times Jesus and God say, "Fear not . . .", for instance. The second reason is that the same point might be relevant in a different scenario, and so mentioning it again in a different context is required. I suggest making a mental note of these repetitions, as it may help you to take note of what is being emphasised, or indeed, the different context for its usage.

I suggest you go into this book expectantly, but without any preconceived ideas. What I mean by this is that you should expect that God is going to move into a relationship with you, but that you should have no expectations as to *how* He will, *what* it will feel like, *when* it will happen, etc. All too often I want to "plan" it all or put God in a box (place parameters around Him), and when we do this, He simply steps back and waits for us to finish. This level of expectation becomes another expression of our self-will. Oswald Chambers wrote:

When we are certain of the way God is going to work, He will never work that way anymore.[2]

Here is a very important suggestion to remember during this process, and indeed in life: when all else fails, trying to help another person with whatever they may need done, may save the day. The reason I believe this, is that our true problem is self-centredness. Ego, pride and self[3] sometimes consume me to the point where contact with God is just not possible. Most often we are not even aware of this, and we may just feel an uneasiness or pain. By trying to help another I am able to "get out of myself", and in that time there is enough levelling of pride for God to be able to step past my self-will and help me. Try making a point of actively looking for *any* situation where you can help (like holding the door open for someone – whatever presents itself at the time), and never tell anyone else what you have done. It sounds funny, but that is exactly how it worked for me.

Finally, I suggest you enjoy the process, have fun, be relaxed – laugh at yourself; you're funny! As long as you

---

2. Oswald Chambers, *My Utmost for His Highest* (Barbour and Company Inc., 2012), p.156.
3. Read the explanation of the connection between these attitudes at the bottom of page 43.

remain sincere in your desire to have an intimate personal relationship with God, He will be there to meet you. May the Lord our God do for you what you could not do for yourself.

PART ONE

Understanding and Relating

The Breakthrough

My Miracle

(written in September 2008; edited in 2020)

My father became a Christian when I was three years old, he became an ordained minister a few years later, and I have grown up in a Christian home ever since.

I made my personal commitment to God at age eight, was baptized at twelve years old, went to church twice a week, went to youth on Fridays, did an Alpha course, Homiletics course, Hermeneutics course, and was made chairman of the SCA (Students' Christian Association) in my final school year. I once witnessed my dad cast a demon out of a woman, for real. In all this time, though, nothing special had ever happened for *me*. I remember asking my mother why miracles never happened to us. She just said that they did in all sorts of little ways, but in my mind, I just put it down to chance and not actual miracles. So, I knew there was power, and that God was there, but it seemed He was just not available for me. This is why I have called this story "My Miracle".

I remember feeling different from everybody else at the tender young age of three. I went to a nursery school from this age and remember all the kids wearing woollen mittens when the winter came.

I thought, "I gotta get me a pair of these gloths [gloves]."

So, I went home and asked my mum if she could knit me a pair. She asked me what colour and I said dark green, my favourite colour, and she proceeded to knit me a beautiful pair of dark green woollen gloves. According to my mum, I looked at them a little apprehensively and asked why these gloves had so many "fingers". She realized then that I had wanted mittens and said that she was sure some of the other kids would have "fingered" gloves and not to worry.

Off I went to school sporting my new dark green gloves, only to run into hordes of kids all wearing mittens! As kids can do, they laughed and teased me a bit, but it shattered me! I felt devastated and shameful inside, out of place and *different!* I took them off, threw them in the bin and sat in the sandpit crying. I was burning inside with humiliation, and this turned to anger at the other kids. Believe it or not, I started skipping nursery school by hiding in a bush at the bottom of the garden. My mum's feisty friend in her clapped-out old white Peugeot 504 would come to take me to school, but when I didn't appear after she tooted her horn a few times, she would drive on. A little later I would go indoors and tell my mum that I had been waiting but the woman hadn't turned up.

This feeling of being the odd one out persisted throughout my schooling; the continual feeling that I never quite fitted in, that all the other kids were "normal" and that I had to do my best to become "normal" and fit in. So, I used to try all sorts of weird shenanigans to be accepted or noticed; I guess what people would call showing off. I see now that this just added fuel to the fire. I never did things deliberately to be *different*, most of the time it was because I wasn't sure about something, because I could not remember, or I had not been listening properly. For instance, if there was a sports day and the kids were all in vests, I would inevitably rock up in a T-shirt. If black shorts were the order of the day, guess what? I would be wearing a nifty pair of dark blue shorts. One of my peers may say something like, "Ha, ha, ha! Look! Rory's parents must be colour blind or something!" To hide the embarrassment, fear turned to anger, and I'd hit him. I would get into trouble and the other kids seemed to dislike me even more. I sat once more outside the circle of normality feeling very sorry for myself.

I just couldn't get it; I did well at sports, got good grades and generally did all the things that seemed right and yet I felt so disconnected from all the other kids around. Looking back now, it sends shivers down my spine when I realize the power of perception. The real truth, I think, was that I was just like all the other kids, and they actually didn't consider me too different from the rest; they teased each other equally. The difference was in the way I felt about myself. What I now realize is that this feeling is *ego*. One of the best definitions of ego that I have ever heard was by an A.A. member, Chuck C[4], who said that ego was . . .

. . . *the feeling of conscious separation from God, good and life.*

---

4. Chuck 'C' or Charles Chamberlain, passed away in 1984, but some of his shares were recorded at AA meetings on a retreat at Pala Mesa in 1975.

That was me! This, I believe, made me a prime candidate for a reliance on something *else* to make me feel connected.

During my high-school years, I started to resent all the "hypocrites" in the church. As most are, I was no fool and carefully analysed the church situation in the grander scheme of things. We went to an extremely charismatic church, which started to look more and more like a show to me. I look back now and I realize that it was probably because I never felt any real connection with God. I think if I had, other people's ways might not have affected me as badly as they did. For instance, I observed the same elderly lady in her pink and white floral dress, go to the front for prayer almost every Sunday. Every time the pastor laid his hand on her forehead, she would keel over backwards in as graceful a swoon as was possible. I always felt for the poor church usher who had to "wrestle" her and lay her down in as dignified a manner as possible! There would be the ones who would start speaking in tongues and everybody would get fully involved: chanting, wailing and singing in different tongues. It would always end in a mass crescendo and then die down for the preaching.

I never felt anything in all this. I wanted to "feel" something and took my turn to get prayed for. But when the pastor prayed for me to receive the Holy Spirit and to speak in tongues, I felt him steadily trying to ease me off my feet with the palm of his hand against my forehead. I stood my ground and pushed with my forehead! He said I was resisting the power of the Holy Spirit entering me – the manifestation of which would be that I would be able to speak in tongues. I said that he was trying to push me over. He got highly irate and told me that I had a spirit of rebellion in me. I thought he was a schmuck! The people in the church would often talk about the "ones who had received the Holy Spirit" – basically those of the congregation that could speak in tongues, as opposed to the ones that couldn't – in what came across to me as a sort of spiritual hierarchy. It seemed they viewed the ones who couldn't speak in tongues as not quite having "arrived" – not godly enough. This was my perception at the time.[5]

I remember feeling very hurt, shamed, rejected and once more "out". I thought straight away that this stood to reason, as I *was* different, remember? I had so badly wanted to "receive the Holy Spirit" and feel some sort of real connection to God that I did everything I thought I was supposed to do. I thought it was that problem of "being different" that kept me out of it, and I couldn't stand the feeling of shame.

I vowed there and then that when I left home, I would never go back to church if I could possibly help it. I couldn't "get the Holy Spirit" in me, and I wasn't considered for miracles by God, and I felt ashamed of not being able to be *normal* with these Christian people. I hated the feeling of pretending that I had a connection with God when truly, I had no feeling of connection at all.

Things changed after the army when I moved to Johannesburg – the big city – to study. I had finished school and was conscripted into the South African Defence Force for a year. I left the idea of God behind; I felt it was easier this way for me. After the army, I studied Haematology

---

5. Today I can gladly say that the Holy Spirit's power is operating in my life, and that speaking in tongues is very much part of my daily prayer life.

(Medical Tech.), and a lot of our practical exams were done at Wits University. It was there that I found that missing "something" that had kept me from being normal and connecting properly with others. It was a "Magic Muti" (Zulu word for medicine) called booze. When I had had a drink or two, the most amazing thing happened to me! A warm, "fuzzy", self-contented feeling enveloped my entire body from head to toe. It gave my mind a rest from worrying whether I fitted in or not. It unleashed my tongue that was laced with wit, charm and an exceptional vocabulary that must have been hidden in me all along! The effects were incredible; I was the joke-telling funny guy, the daredevil, the friendly guy, the philosopher and . . . the *lover!* All the guys liked me, and the girls seemed to take a keen interest in me as well. But the most important revelation for me was that I felt *connected,* like I fitted in properly for the first time ever! I could even get up on the bar counter, drop my pants and "moon" the crowd and still feel very normal. It became a *must* thing I did with all the lads – *my* group! I was never able to make a connection with God, but this booze allowed me to feel *real* and truly connected with those around me.

I gave this phenomenon some serious thought, and eventually sold myself on an idea. I was suffering with some kind of chemical imbalance that caused me to act stupid and weird, and that was why people couldn't accept me. When I consumed a few drinks, something about the alcohol managed to right this chemical imbalance and this allowed me to function and feel normal. Clearly after that, people were responding to me positively as they would do anyone else. I was sure there was some medication that a doctor could prescribe for me that would do the same thing, but why should I change a winning formula? Meanwhile, to keep my confidence up to continue with this circus act, I was consuming more and more.

My drinking built up over the next five years to a point where friends did not want me around; I was generally disruptive and obnoxious. This then awakened the old feeling of being left out, which, in turn, awoke three terrible "demons" which would haunt me for a long time to come: Rejection, Fear and Resentment . . .

I changed my friends and started to hang out with people who drank the same as me and whose social standards weren't as high as those of my other friends. However, I still let that unrighteous indignation seethe within me – they had left me out and pushed me away. I drank more and I drank hard.

My morals started to be wain; stupid flings, drugs, lying, verbal abuse towards others, fights and laziness. This would make me feel even more morose.

I started to justify my behaviour by convincing myself that it was always someone else who had caused me to react with whichever inappropriate behaviour I had done. There were numerous secret attempts to connect with God quite sincerely, but I never felt any connection. It was strange, there seemed to be a blockage of sorts.

At this stage, my father was telling me I was an alcoholic, and I fought him all the way on that one. He had said that I was a "raging alcoholic" and that I would never be able to touch booze again. I guess that's why I fought him so fervently. How was I going to feel normal without my "Magic Muti"? The other reason was that he always had to be right, and I wanted to prove him wrong. But I was worried – I knew that, somehow, I had a problem that needed attention. I just felt too "tired" all the time to address it.

When I did pluck up the courage to address the problem, I was twenty-eight years old; it was the year 2000. I went to a psychiatrist and told him I was hitting the bottle a little too heavily, and that I wanted to stop for three months. The real reason I wanted to stop for three months was to prove to my father that I wasn't an alcoholic. After keeping off the alcohol for three months, I hit the bottle with a vengeance! Within a week or so, I was right back where I started.

Before I moved down to the Kwa-Zulu Natal South Coast on a big building project, I had an argument with my mother about a disturbance I'd caused with her neighbour. She wrote me a letter saying she loved me but that I was not welcome at her house anymore. This affected me very badly. The guilt ate at me terribly! But, being a true alcoholic, I drank more and put the cause of the argument down to my mother being stubborn. The reason it hurt me so much is that my mother is one of the sweetest people I know. The guilt and depression were almost unbearable! This all happened to me in October 2004.

Then, on 12th July 2005, my nineteen-year-old sister was tragically killed in a car accident with her boyfriend. A while after this happened, I was drinking one rainy day (no work, supposedly) at 12 noon, and getting completely "blotto". One of the plumbers that knew me came in and asked how I could be so drunk so early. My reply still disgusts me today. I said, "My nineteen-year-old sister was killed in a car accident!" He humbly apologized, bought me a drink and left. As I raised the drink to my lips, a thought struck me – it was already ten months after her death! How low can a person go? I was literally using my sister's death as an excuse to sit and get drunk in the middle of the day. I had convinced myself that this was why I was drinking and that I needed it to get through this tough time.

In my mind I had reached the end. I tried all the tricks in the book to stop drinking, but I could not. This *thing* had me; I was now 100 per cent sure that I could not stop drinking or even moderate it. The fear of this realization was almost unbearable. I could not keep this pretence up any longer. The pretence I wanted everyone to see was that things were under control. I hated everything about myself, and it was getting worse! I couldn't bear hurting people anymore, but I kept doing it.

Around this time, I met a lad at the pub who never drank. He was a 2-handicap golfer and used to come in and play a golf machine game in the pub, but he only ever drank Coke. The funny thing was that he seemed very normal and quite at ease.

I caught up with Daniel M a week or so later. It was a Sunday, late afternoon, on 28th May 2006, and I was "on like a scone"; merrily drunk! I asked him if he used to drink before, as I noticed he never drank, and he confirmed that he had in the past. I then asked him how that all worked.

He replied, "I'm an alcoholic and I go to meetings on a Monday and Tuesday night each week."

I then asked if he thought I was an alcoholic, and he told me he couldn't answer that question. I asked him that if he, after going to meetings, couldn't tell me if I was an alcoholic, how was I going to know? I thought to myself that that was quite a good question, but Daniel just smiled and shrugged and said I had to come to that conclusion on my own.

The next morning there was a knock at my door at about 10.30am. Daniel barged in, slapped a dark blue paperback on the kitchen nook and said, "Read that! Answer the questions in that brochure, but don't tell me what your answers are because I don't want to know! Oh yes, use a pencil because you are going to lie, then you can do it again when you decide to be honest! Cheers"; and he was gone. His "enthusiasm" still makes me chuckle years later!

I marked twelve out of twenty questions "yes" and felt quite chuffed with myself, until I read the bottom piece: "If you have answered YES to any three or more, you are definitely an alcoholic." To back up this bold claim of theirs, it added in brackets, "The above Test Questions are used by John Hopkins University, Baltimore, MD, in deciding whether or not a patient is an alcoholic." A huge breakthrough occurred there and then; I became convinced in my mind that I was an alcoholic! I had toyed with that thought many times before, but now I knew.

I read Bill W's story at the beginning of that dark blue book *(Alcoholics Anonymous)*. The second breakthrough occurred here; my story was identical to his! Not in the events or anything, but in his description of how he felt and perceived things. This story had been written over seventy years earlier, so no one could be trying to pull the wool over my eyes. We must have been feeling the same. Bill W got sober; maybe I could too. Excitement and hope gripped me as I read the pages. This was mind-blowing stuff here, I thought, until I saw the fourth chapter entitled, WE AGNOSTICS!

"Here we go again with this religious stuff!" I thought. I wanted to turf the whole thing. I had done the whole "God and church" thing and had failed miserably at experiencing anything real with Him. The God I thought I knew was not going to help me with this drinking problem. But I believe that the first paragraph or so saved my life. It said that the Program was not a religious one but rather a deeply spiritual one. It said that we should keep our minds open to the fact that there might be a being greater than ourselves who could possibly be able to help. Reading this made me just curious enough to read on. I praise God that I pressed on with reading the book. It suggested that instead of listening to other people's perceptions of who God is, why didn't I choose my own perception of Him? They hinted at the idea of thinking of God as one's *own*, not as other people's God. I decided my God would be loving, forgiving, understanding, patient, graceful, supportive, able and *real* to me. When I look at a portrait of Jesus these days, He is all those things and more! The only thing I had to do was give Him the problem with complete abandon. I am now very grateful to God for the gift of desperation. I was so desperate that I was willing to try anything! I know that I would not have gone through with the Program so wholeheartedly if I were not frantically desperate. I knew I was beaten and could not stop, so I let go and, amazingly, I did stop.

I chose the only God I'd ever vaguely known, the heavenly Father, and said this to Him with all sincerity (which, indecently, I had done on numerous occasions before):

"God, if you're there, I need a miracle. My problem is that I can't stop drinking so I'm giving you the problem. I am not going to try; I'm just going to read this book a few times. If I feel like a drink tomorrow, I will just go to the bar and make sure it's a triple, because I can't fight it anymore. I will go to one meeting a week if I can, and I will be as honest as I can. I will do whatever they suggest I do at the meetings as best I know how, but You've gotta help because I cannot do it alone."

Little did I know at the time that from that moment on, I would never feel like a drink again. I climbed into bed and slept soundly. The next day I didn't feel like a drink, but that was normal for me after a three-day bender. I asked God to "please help me not to drink today" and I read some of the book. That evening I thanked Him for helping me through the day. The next day, no cravings and I repeated the same pattern as the day before. This carried on and I continued to read; sometimes just a few pages, but mostly a few chapters a day because it was so interesting. I couldn't believe how much sense it all made and how I could relate to each and every story written. I finished the book thrice in five weeks and told Daniel I wanted to go to a meeting.

The first meeting I attended was on 3rd July 2006 in Margate, and I had been sober for exactly five weeks. Daniel said that I should not worry if it didn't make sense in the beginning, but I found that it made perfect sense to me right from the start. I was still reeling in the amazement at the fact that I wasn't the only one who felt "different" and drank to try to feel normal.

The next night I went to another meeting in Port Shepstone, where one of the members was celebrating his fifteenth year sober. I couldn't believe it! I thought that if I made three months it would be incredible. I listened to his story and, once again, it was very similar to my own experience. Two things were said at that meeting, one by him and one by another member, which has stuck with me. He said to me, "You are the most important person at this meeting. We think you can do more for us than we can do for you; you remind us of what it was like for us before. So, take the cotton wool out of your ears and stick it in your mouth. In other words, shut up and listen!" *I'm the most important person there and I'm told to shut up and listen!?* Another guy with three years' sobriety said, "Just make sure you keep coming back. The meeting you least feel like attending is the one you most need to be at."

I followed both these pieces of advice and, boy, am I glad I did! They told me to get a sponsor (mentor), so I got three – Daniel M, Blackie H and Rajan I. I owe these men my life. I thank God for giving them to me to be there for me. Raj said to me, "This is a suggestive Program . . . *so we suggest you do it!*" I still laugh at that today and share it at many of my talks. This was how I was introduced to the Program, and I started doing it as best I could.

Three months came along, and I was very scared a couple of days before 29th August. I knew that this would be the longest stretch without a drink in seventeen years. The lads at the group rallied around me with support, jokes and love. I spoke to my God through the Lord Jesus to comfort me, and He did. The day came and went, and I realized then that someone else was in control, that on 29th May 2006, my God granted me my miracle! He finally connected with me. I can't describe the euphoria I felt when I realized

His power, love and amazing grace had been granted me. I felt peace, contentment and excitement at this new-found awakening. I had not realized it before, but He was simply there with me – as real and intimate as a normal person I was friends with – and I knew it from the pit of my stomach to be true. Without a doubt, it is the most incredible experience in my life to date.

The farmer-evangelist Angus Buchan likes to say, "In order for a miracle to occur, the situation must not be difficult; it must be impossible!"[6] I now know this to be true and realize that what my mum said was correct: miracles did happen to me every day. I could have been in serious trouble or killed on many occasions acting thoughtlessly while inebriated.

He had never left me through all those times, even though I'd given up on Him – what an awesome God! Looking back, I can honestly say that I am grateful to be an alcoholic. I don't believe I would have been able to find a relationship with God any other way. I have learned so many amazing things that I realize I never would have learned had I not been an alcoholic. It has taught me a new way of thinking; a selfless Christ-like style of living. A very simple phrase mentioned many times in meetings by my Christian alcoholic sponsor Blackie H, has become part of my daily prayer. He says, "Just for today, I want to help somebody. But the big secret is, nobody must know about it!" This so encapsulates a Jesus-modelled Christianity. I have found the following to be true by following that simple phrase:

---

6. Angus Buchan is a farmer and evangelist who I met on his farm in Greytown, KZN, South Africa, at a couple of conventions he held.

- It helps me live in the present and focus on what I can do right now.

- It helps me obey the Lord's Word (Holy Bible), and thereby fulfil my purpose of glorifying and worshipping Him.

- It assists someone else in need.

- It takes away my self-centredness because I'm focused on someone else. This in turn takes away any guilt, depression, anxiety and self-pity I might have had. How can you have any of these feelings when you're not focused on yourself?

- It keeps my motives pure. If no one knows that I've helped someone, I can't be applauded.

- I store treasure in heaven, where it counts most, because God sees my heart is true.

Even if this phrase is not understood for all its benefits, the person applying it to their lives will still have a different outlook on life. They will still reap the reward of serenity in their lives, as an unexplainable peace and contentment envelops them. This is the power of the Lord that enveloped me because I was prepared to "let go and let God". This was the door through which God entered into a real relationship with me because I had finally learnt how to open it to Him.

In these years that have gone by, I have learned so much and many amazing things have happened for me. I still have to fight resentment (the number-one destroyer of a deep relationship with God), expectations, anger, fear, frustrations, self-centredness and trying to take back control from God. But when I get it right, and I have many slips in-between, He blesses me with an inner peace and joy, and I can truly feel His presence. This Program is a journey, and that's exciting because there is always something to do, with new challenges every day. The thing I really like about it is that I don't have to do it alone anymore; He is *always* there with me.

There was an old man from one of the groups who has subsequently passed away, and he often used to say, "You youngsters that are new here, stick around – things beyond your wildest dreams will come true!" Boy, was he right! I have been able to make and save some good money. I have been single the whole time, but I've recently started dating the most amazing woman in the world. She loves the Lord like I do, and I know the Lord will honour us as we obey and honour His word.[7] I never asked for these things at the time. Instead, as was suggested to me, I have prayed for humility, honesty, love, perseverance and the knowledge and power to do His will for my life.

> *But seek ye first the kingdom of God, and his righteousness; and all these things shall be added unto you.* Matthew 6:33

> *Give, and it shall be given unto you; good measure, pressed down, and shaken together, and running over, shall men give into your bosom. For with the same measure that ye mete withal it shall be measured to you again.* Luke 6:38

---

7. Pauline is currently my wife of many happy years, and counting . . .

After reading these two passages, I know that God has been truthful in fulfilling His word in my life.

It is a very simple Program, yet I always want to complicate things! Christianity is the same; it is very simple but with huge rewards. I want to have a closer relationship with God. I believe that He wants this and that is why He created us. We are created so that God may demonstrate His love, and that is just incredible. I feel very humbled when I think how small and insignificant I am, how much I've hurt the Lord, and yet He still wants a relationship with me. I want to help people, and I believe that God Himself has put that desire in my heart. I try to commit myself to this cause by the strength and opportunities He affords me, and my motivation is that I love God and I want to show Him gratitude for what He has done in my life. To me, when I help someone for nothing in return, this is gratitude in action – the unconscious reward is peace, comfort and joy with myself. All the praise, honour and glory be to the Lord our God! Amen.

The Question

Why can't I?

I have personally asked this question hundreds of times before; to myself, to God, and sometimes to others I may feel have an answer. Why can't I experience a real relationship with God, why do I always feel as if He is aloof and detached from me? Thirty-three years later I found the answer: it is *Pride, Ego, Self.*[8]

I hope this does not seem too harsh and I am certainly not in a position to say whether you have issues of pride, ego

---

8. Throughout the book I will often refer to these three together, as they are very closely related and, in certain contexts, even synonymous. All of them have one key element that is destructive: they are all self-focused. I believe that this element is the biggest problem facing people, and the main hindrance to an intimate relationship with God. Even if you cannot see all three of these issues in yourself, you might be able to identify one or two of them. For example, you might not consider yourself to be proud, but perhaps you can admit that you have a bit of an ego. "Self" is an attitude of, "This is all about me", and the trouble with this attitude is that most often it is sub-conscious, therefore the person is unaware of their self-focus. Sometimes the book will use words such as "self-centredness" or "selfishness". Ego means (quoting Charles Chamberlain from his talks at the Pala Mesa retreat in 1975), "The feeling of conscious separation from God (in other words their creator), good (being able to do the right thing in any given circumstance) and life (the normal everyday things people do and are involved in)." This kind of thinking is very self-centred; effectively it is saying, "I am a very special case – different from the entire universe by being so good/bad/different." This is also a form of pride. In this book, the word "pride" means thinking, "I am more special than anyone else, and therefore in a category of persons all on my own." Again, such thinking is self-centred. Here, "pride" has nothing to do with one's dignity, which is a different meaning of the word. So, in summary, "self" focuses on "I" and believes my situation to be unique ("ego") and supremely different from others ("pride").

or self in your life; only you will be able to figure that out through the process. However, if you find yourself unable to experience a real or strong relationship with God, it might show a sincere desire on your part if you go through this book prayerfully and see what you find. This is exactly what I did. This process you are now on is the solution to *uncovering* all this for you, so that you can evaluate for yourself. You will then be able to *truthfully* discover what is really there. Once this happens and you see the truth, you will learn how to *discard* that which is making God feel so "out of touch" for you. If you feel it does not relate to you, then you can leave it. I do not believe that this is the only solution to establishing a truly heart-felt relationship with God, but it is the only solution that worked in my life.

I may now sound a bit philosophical, but I would like to reiterate that I am no expert and that these thoughts came to me via reading and experience; through the Holy Spirit, I believe.

I have been told so many times that I had a drinking problem. I later found out that the truth was that it was really *my* solution that had stopped working. This brings me to the point of what I call dependencies. There are dependency disorders, which are unnatural and generally follow a pattern of obsessive behaviour (alcoholism, drugs, sex, pornography, over-eating, gambling, etc.). However, these are not the only dependency disorders, as anything we end up doing obsessively or depending on to make us feel a sense of ease and comfort, I believe, is a dependency disorder (overworking or over exercising, obsession with a partner or child, etc.). Depending heavily on other people or *things* to fill in something missing in your life, or to ease feelings of fear, rejection, restlessness, irritability, or discontentment, is ultimately not healthy. I have found this to be true for me because they are all fallible, and therefore destined to let us down at some point. These people or other things I had relied on may have given me a semblance of ease and comfort in the past, but because it may not be working so well now, a form of insanity takes over and I start to subconsciously repeat the same process over and over again, resulting in the same outcome of disappointment each time. One of the main reasons for this insane repetition, I believe, is because I have not found or experienced anything else that has ever really worked. What I am saying is, if we turn to and *rely* heavily on *any* other source for comfort, peace, fulfilment, etc., other than the Lord, we are in danger of creating a dependency. These things become a crutch to support us, and because we don't know any better, or how to let these things go, we cannot connect to the awesome peace and security that an intimate relationship with God brings. If we do depend on our spouse, for instance, or our child gives us an immense sense of love and fulfilment, we need to still make sure that we are consciously acknowledging that this is actually coming from God as a blessing through this person.

Proverbs 3:5-6 says, *"Trust in the Lord with all thine heart; and lean not unto thine own understanding. In all thy ways acknowledge him, and he shall direct thy paths."*

I believe that our inherent nature stems from how God created us. God created us to be obsessive over Him, to seek safety and security and comfort and peace and fulfilment and all those good things from Him. The original sin of the archangel Lucifer was *self*; pride, if you like:

45

Your heart was proud because of your beauty; you corrupted your wisdom for the sake of your splendour. I cast you to the ground; I exposed you before kings, to feast their eyes on you. Ezekiel 28:17 (ESV)

Our natural fleshly nature was corrupted when the devil (the fallen archangel Lucifer) caused Eve to sin. Since then, we have been living with a fleshly nature that is corrupted and easily swayed from the truth. The lie and deceit the devil brought against man was something he aimed at our pride. He was basically saying that God helped me a lot, but did I really need to be *totally* dependent on Him all the time, implying that surely, I had enough of my own strength and ability not to have to totally surrender *everything* to God. As the devil always does, he blinded me from the truth that everything I was and am, came from God – every breath I took was because God had ordained it so. My underlying God-given nature is still to depend upon worshipping and being in close relation to God. This pride that has crept in has distorted my focus from God, and I naturally start to cling to other things for ease, and to comfort those restless, uneasy, discontent feelings that crop up. I believe that these feelings stem from how God made us and are actually there to alert us to when we are not in proper relationship with our Creator. The Deceiver (Satan) has corrupted these feelings by distorting the truth through pride. God will not be in proper relationship with us if He is not the centre of our desires and our lives.

However, although we live the lie[9] in our lives more often than not, the truth is that the devil is already defeated

9. The lie that we are not yet redeemed, and that we do not stand righteous in God's sight through the blood of Jesus shed on the cross (Colossians 1:13-14).

(Hebrews 2:14), and we are already victorious with what Jesus did on the cross. All that happens now is that our weakened "flesh" believes the lie the devil repeatedly tells, and we succumb to it.

There is one other thing I would like to touch on from my personal experience. I have discovered this in my nature and have also noticed it as being a general character trait in many others I have worked through the Program with, and I believe it may really help you. As I have said, keep an open mind, but if you feel it is not something you relate to, you can just discard it; it won't have a negative impact on the process.

What I've come to understand, is how very touchy we are. I believe that we are extremely sensitive people. This can be a very positive attribute as far as showing empathy towards other people goes – not so nice when I think someone is having a go at me. This happens more often than not without any malice from the other person. For example, my boss comes to check my building site and informs me that he would like me to tidy the site up a bit as it is looking messy. Immediately, the thought flashes through my mind, "What does he mean? Is he trying to imply that I'm a messy person, that I can't do my job? Does he know how much pressure we're under with that breakdown?" The fact of the matter is that he does understand; he is not necessarily cross, he is merely doing his job and pointing out something that needs attention. I often grab hold of this big, fat, juicy resentment to comfort me, and my subsequent attitude afterwards leaves a lot to be desired. The resulting attitude meant I was often treading on dangerous ground, as my reaction to this resentment could cost me my job. But more than this is that it cuts me off from God.

But if ye do not forgive, neither will your Father which is in heaven forgive your trespasses.   Mark 11:26[10]

Unforgiveness is something that will instantly cut you off from relationship with God, and I believe that resentment is the number one reason for unforgiveness. In my life this was a huge issue, as I really viewed my resentments as justified. I had these resentments from very young, as you have read, and this set me up for a good thirty years of not being able to be in true relation with God (remember not to confuse your salvation with being in relationship with God – they are two separate things). I speak about this more in depth later on and, praise God, there is an actual workable solution to trace resentments that are possibly hidden from our lives today.

---

10. You will not find this verse in all Bible translations, so if you have a version without it, you will find a similar reading in Matthew 6:15.

The Blockage Dilemma

Knowing and understanding why I cannot seem to move into a real and intimate relationship with God is a start. I truly believe that pride, self, ego and resentment (unforgiveness), are the things that cut us off from an intimate relationship with God. Knowing and understanding this, I still found it impossible to get rid of any of these things, no matter how hard I tried; knowledge and understanding was not enough, not by a long shot.

In my life, until I worked through the steps of the Program, I was totally blind to my self-centredness. I've heard a brilliant saying, "A person cannot see ... until they can *see.*" It seems such a silly saying, but so true when you think about it. I remember people saying to me how selfish and self-centred I was. This came especially from my father who was always around and close to me. It really used to irk me as a youngster when he pointed this out to me. What did he know? There is a another saying I remember, "If there is anything in life you want to know, ask a teenager and they'll tell you!" I was exactly like that. In my mind, my problem wasn't self-centredness, it was a lack of understanding on the part of other people. I had a massive ego and thought I was destined for great things. I was a genius with huge potential, and I could not understand why other people could not see it. If they were able to see and understand my potential, they would make me captain of the rugby team, or send me overseas to represent the school in debating. My ego never allowed me to just be in the team, I had to be captain; as far as I was concerned, my teammates needed good-quality leadership, and I was their man! I felt hard done by; all the others seemed to get the breaks except me. I was always overlooked, and so I set about rectifying the status quo. Now, I would probably say that my illustration of ego is more of an extreme example, and that your example may be significantly milder and more subtle. Nevertheless, it can still be enough to cause a blockage between you and a relationship with God.

It is not easy for us to get rid of self-will – this ego – mainly because we cannot see it. It is a phenomenon, but I believe that those who suffer with pride-ego-self, can never see it in themselves, even though they can see it so clearly in others. I couldn't see it in myself.

I thank God that there is a simple solution to this malady, the one found in this Program. We will, however, need continual maintenance, which I'm happy to say is also contained in this process. As was said by the late Chuck C in his talks at the Pala Mesa retreat in 1975, and with which I wholeheartedly agree:

"I believe that we can never fully tame or control the human ego. It is a continual daily surrender."

For me, it is my cross that I must take up daily (Luke 9:23). I am so grateful to God that I saw this after thirty-three years. It is easy to tell when the ego is rising; I feel uneasy and the pain returns. When we are in this state, God cannot help us. This is where self-will starts to take over. When that happens, I go straight to what the Program says and rectify the situation. In order for me to start dealing with the main problem of self, I *had* to be rid of any other crutches; the main one for me was alcohol, but I had others.

In a nutshell, my dilemma was twofold; I lacked power to overcome feelings of restlessness, irritability, discontentedness, fear, guilt, rejection, and all the other feelings that may stem from these. I had unwittingly turned to people, places or things that gave me temporary relief, but these *things* had stopped working, yet somehow, I felt continually compelled to go back to them regularly. What I came to realize was that I needed a sincere, intimate relationship with God to relieve me of these feelings, as only He had the true power to overcome them. In order to have this kind of relationship with God, I had to be rid of the other things I had depended on, but I lacked the power to be able to really let go of them. God had the power, but I could not get into relationship with Him because of the very thing I needed to be rid of. This is the first dilemma.

The second part of the dilemma was that I needed to be rid of *self* in order to have a relationship with God, but it is my very selfishness that prevents me from seeing this. When I finally do see this, I find that I do not have the willpower required to change.

Basically, I find that I am totally powerless to remove self or the crutches in order for me to be able to move into a sincere intimate relationship with God so that His true unfailing power would be there to help me live peacefully, joyfully and comfortably with myself – this is a very frightening realization to have. Please try to not lose hope; there is a real solution to these dilemmas. Let's read on . . .

God's Spiritual Order

I have found that God has a very definite set of priorities for us, an *order* if you like, and this can all be found in His operational manual for human beings – the Bible.

I was totally self-absorbed and all I could think about was myself and ways to better my situation. I really could not see just how selfish I was, and it hurt me badly when people told me so. What's wrong with looking after "number one"? After all, if everyone did that, the world would surely be a better place? Through experience, I do not believe this to be true.

First of all, we as people generally seem to be totally absorbed with looking after ourselves – I most definitely include myself in this "we". Now I'm not speaking of prudence here, which, I believe through reading the Bible, God considers a valuable virtue.

I believe it all has to do with our design, our make-up. I have a beautiful illustration, which I believe came to me from the Lord. You will read all about my sequestration[11] later on in the book, but one of the things my wife and I needed to do was buy a car in her name. The blessings

---

11. Declaration of insolvency.

God places on us are truly awesome sometimes. Through a friend, we were able to buy a diesel Audi for a good price and in an immaculate condition. We had had a petrol car before, which the bank was going to come and reclaim. I remember going to fill the new car up and reading "Diesel Only" written somewhere. It took me back to a time once when a petrol attendant had put petrol into the tank of a friend's car that had a diesel engine. My friend drove a little way with the car jerking and spluttering until it cut out and stalled at the side of the road. We had to get it towed to a garage where they drained the petrol and flushed out the engine before they put in diesel and my friend could fetch his car. What a waste of time and money! I thought to myself how nice this Audi looked and how fast it could go. I realized, though, that it would go nowhere if I filled it with petrol, never mind how good it looked or what potential it had. I had always preferred petrol cars; they were quieter and didn't smoke as much. I had the habit of always putting petrol in my car, and if I hadn't seen the sign that said, "Diesel Only", I would probably have put in petrol. You see, the manufacturers of this car designed it to run on diesel. I cannot argue with them and say that they are "mental", that I'll be putting in petrol anyway because that's what I like. It doesn't matter what I like or dislike; if I put petrol in, the car will *not perform*.

It dawned on me that I had previously being trying to "drive" my own life in this way. You see, before I accepted Jesus, I had been an old petrol car that had been going on petrol the whole time. This "petrol" was actually my self-will. When I accepted Jesus' death on the cross and believed in His resurrecting power at the age of eight, I became born again and had effectively been made a "new car". Only, this one ran on diesel. This new life doesn't run on self-will; it runs on *His will*. This "diesel", or God's will, we run on is the new commandment:

Thou shalt love the Lord thy God with all thy heart, and with all thy soul, and with all thy strength, and with all thy mind; and thy neighbour as thyself. Luke 10:27

How do I best love Him? It is by trusting and obeying Him. In order for me to obey Him, I have to know what He wants, and I find this in His instruction manual, the Bible. For me, one of the most profound instructions given to us by God is found in Matthew 28:19-20:

Go ye therefore, and teach all nations, baptizing them in the name of the Father, and of the Son, and of the Holy Ghost: Teaching them to observe all things whatsoever I have commanded you: and, lo, I am with you always, even unto the end of the world. Amen.

It must be remembered that this commission was given to the disciples after they had received Jesus' teaching. I have learnt in life that we cannot give away what we don't have. What we have received, we should freely give away. God created everything, so we cannot love Him by getting Him a bunch of flowers or giving Him a big hug. The way we can love Him is by obeying what He tells us to do, and that is basically to pass on to other people what has been so freely given us by God through His grace.

We must bear in mind that as we do His will and help others, the result in others' lives is not all that important to us. We cannot "save" them; only God can. It works just as much the other way in that we cannot damn them either. It doesn't have much to do with us and the other person at all, actually; it is all about God and His relationship with me. We move into a relationship with God at this point, and this is God's greatest desire; to be in a personal relationship with His creation – us! This is just awesome that this mighty God wants to be in a relationship with "little ol' me". It's much bigger, but similar, to an ordinary person being invited to have dinner with the Head of State. When I am doing God's will and helping others, my engine purrs, and the car cruises. I am at one with my creator. I am filled with peace, joy and contentment. This is how we are designed to function, and it is no good getting angry with The Manufacturer. This is God's spiritual order.

In the next chapter we will discuss more about what it means to actually be able to effectively let go of these things and let God take over; these principles and understandings really helped prepare my heart and mind for the process to follow, and I found the insight quite exciting.

Letting Go and Letting God

Pain

I was about five or six years old, I guess, when we moved into a new house in Ladysmith. There were a lot of trees in this garden and I loved climbing trees, but there was one tree that had a bough overhanging the roof, and my father had told me not to climb this one as it was dangerous (the story sounds familiar, doesn't it?). I climbed all the other trees for a while, and then decided to climb the one I was not supposed to.

I climbed up the trunk and went out on the bough hand-over-fist as my legs dangled, until I got stuck about halfway across to the roof. I could not go forwards or backwards, and I'd break my legs or neck if I let go. Panic and fear set in, and I bellowed out to my dad at the top of my voice to come and help. He came running outside and stopped under the bough of the tree and told me to let go and he'd catch me. I started crying at the thought of letting go and him dropping me. He kept reassuring me that he would not let me fall, and that he could only help me if I let go. The bark was cutting into my wrists causing extra pain, and my arms were completely lame, and I realized I had no choice,

I had to let go. *The pain had become too unbearable*, and I was desperate. I closed my eyes, took a deep breath, resigned my fate into my father's hands, and let go. My dad caught me with ease, put me down on my feet, muttered something about how he wished we kids would just use our ears more, and disappeared through the house and into his study. I especially remember thinking to myself how easily he'd caught me. I thought about the worry, trauma, pain and anguish that could have been avoided had I let go straight away.

My recovery was similar to this childhood experience in many ways. I had got myself to a point in my drinking where I knew I could not go backwards or forwards and I couldn't let go, because there was no one to catch me. I couldn't drink because it was destroying me, but I couldn't stop either, because it's all I knew that had worked. I hung there not knowing what to do; I knew I was headed for certain death. When there was this mention of a Program that worked, the pain and desperation had made me willing to try it. In the Program they said at one point that I should hand it over to God and let go. I realized that I was facing the same dilemma as when I was a kid; I didn't believe God would "catch" me if I let go. To this day, I thank God for the gift of desperation the pain brought on. I had no choice anymore but to follow the Program's suggestion and let go, because I was dying and there was no cure – I was now desperate. I closed my eyes, asked Him to take over, resigned my fate into my Father's hands, *and let go*. I have not had the slightest desire to drink since that day on 29th May 2006.

One of my special scriptures is Psalm 37:23-24:

The steps of a good man are ordered by the Lord; and He delighteth in his way. Though he falls, he shall not be utterly cast down: for the Lord upholdeth him with his hand.

I often wonder where I would be if I'd found the Program earlier in my life, but I know that I was far too self-centred and egotistical to ever have listened. God knew I needed the pain to bring enough desperation to actually listen and let go. I thank Him for this, because I would never have been able to establish the relationship I now have with Him without the pain. I am not suggesting that you will need such an extreme case of desperation and pain before there is enough desire for you to do the work; quite the contrary. I believe that most people are not nearly such an extreme case of self-will run riot as I was. If you are reading this book, though, I believe there will be a niggling discomfort or maybe even just an underlying sense of emptiness in your life. You will most certainly sense that there is something missing with your connection to God. I am pleased to say that the spiritual set of tools that have been laid out in the process are exactly the same, no matter which category you may fit into.

In the rest of this chapter, I would like to discuss three fundamental aspects that helped me let go completely. I believe that because humans are so ruled by ego, if we were left like this, we'd be back up that tree and trying the same trick again in a few months' time. Pain, as you've heard, is what brought me to the point of being willing to listen. I am truly hoping and praying that you don't need to get to the point of such pain as I had to. Indeed, there are many who have gone way past my point of desperation before they were willing. However, I sincerely believe that if you can see yourself on this same "train" of *self*, you'll be able to make the decision to get off at a much earlier stop than I did, by the wonderful grace of God – this is my prayer.

Honesty

A definition of honest is "fair and righteous (righteous, meaning morally right and law-abiding) in speech and action – not lying, cheating, or stealing – sincere". I can concur with this in my understanding of what it means now, but I certainly could not have done this in my earlier days. I had the idea that as long as you were not trying to hurt anyone, whatever you said did not matter. Once I had my eyes opened, the magnitude of the level of honesty that was going to be required of me to get through this Program properly was daunting to say the least. We are talking about a level of honesty at which, when I've done something good that has really helped someone, I can ask myself if I was pure enough in my motive. Did I actually do this thing so that others might think of me as a nice guy? Did I do it because it benefitted me in some way? Did this person perhaps do something good to me first, and do I just want to keep this "give and take" relationship going? Did I do it to get out of some kind of trouble? Did I even do it because I felt sorry for them? Or did I do it because I am totally grateful for what God has done in my life; that I truly love Him for who He is, and I want to show that gratitude to Him by passing it on to another person? It is difficult to buy God a bunch of flowers when He's the one who made the flowers, the money and me.

My motive will never become one of helping people unless I can recognize and confess that this has not been my motive.

Another example of the level of honesty I needed is that I had to be able to admit, "I don't understand," "I don't feel that," "I want to do this but I can't bring myself to," "I don't believe in God," "I don't love that girl," "I can't forgive him," "I haven't worked through the steps thoroughly," "I haven't told you everything," "I haven't made my amends properly," "I still resent them," and so on. Silence can also be a lack of honesty. If we want to be honest, we have to be *willing* to follow the recovery Program, admitting we are powerless over being able to be truly honest.

This was the first decision that got the "ball of connecting with God" rolling for me. It was a key factor in breaking down the barrier I had between God and myself. In order for me to connect with God and have a personal relationship with Him, I had to remove the "me" from the equation. For this to happen, I had to humble myself. When I took the first step by becoming as honest as I could about who I was and what my capabilities were, I started to realize I was nothing without God. The bit of talent that had allowed me to learn a few skills in my life so far were from God anyway. Whatever I may achieve, whether it is while following God's plan or not, it could be taken from me in an instant without His protection.[12] Rich, intelligent, successful, handsome men and women have lost things, or

---

12. See Job 1:6 – 2:10.

even their lives, in an instant through forces beyond their control. Honesty brings me to the realization that without God in control of my will, I am set to lose everything.

When we read Jeremiah 5:3, it shows that God is not just casually looking for honesty in us but that he is actually *searching* for it. This implies intensity from God, and intensity shows importance.

The level of importance is such that God struck and crushed His people in order to bring honesty to their lives.[13] The Lord wants fellowship and a relationship with us. This is the reason He created us. Without true honesty, though, there can be no real intimacy in any relationship, let alone with God, and He knows this. We can see here just how much He loves us; it's truly awesome!

"We are not saints." How honest a statement is that! I'll bet anyone is capable of being honest enough to make that statement with belief and conviction. Most of us have probably used it ourselves and heard many others use it too.

No one understands this more than God. The task ahead of us seems tough, as it's not easy to be truly honest. People can be cruel and despising; we could lose face, friends, jobs, families and even spouses. The thought of it strikes fear into most of us; we don't have the strength or fortitude to face this. We have some comfort when we read 1 Corinthians 10:13, as we see that what we're feeling and going through is not unique; others have been through

---

13. Jeremiah 5:3 (NLT) says, "LORD, you are searching for honesty. You struck your people, but they paid no attention. You crushed them, but they refused to be corrected. They are determined, with faces set like stone; they have refused to repent." God was talking to the nation of Israel, but as He has made us His children as well (see 1 John 3); I believe we'd do well to learn from God's response to Israel's dishonesty.

the same. It says that God will not give us more pressure than we can handle and will always provide a way out.

"So now what?" most of us say. How do we find genuine intimacy with God without the essential honesty we are told we need? These were the exact questions I asked when I started the process. From as early as I can remember I had used lying, deceit, manipulation, "candy coating" and even silence to try to get things to benefit me or work my way. It had become a habit, and now I was supposed to just switch over and become totally honest? It just doesn't work that way.

What I did was consciously become as honest as I sincerely knew how, asking the Lord daily for His help, and that was enough for me to get started. *"Amazing!"* you might say. Not really, if you understand that honesty does not come from my efforts, but from God when I trust Him. I found that as I *persisted,* more and more of my untruthful ways came to my attention, and so this mist of lies and deceit began to clear slowly. I found that as I became aware of these lies, I was able to ask God for help and I started telling fewer lies. When I did lie, I felt convicted and made amends as soon as I could.

My prayer used to be short, simple, specific and sincere: *"Lord, please help me to be honest about the facts when telling a story about the fish I caught. In Jesus' name. Amen."* God knows our hearts and wants to give us what we ask for.

If ye then, being evil, know how to give good gifts unto your children, how much more shall your Father which is in heaven give good things to them that ask him?
Matthew 7:11

This scripture shows the character and nature of God, and really gives me hope. Even though we may not receive it all straight away, it *will* happen, just don't stop the daily prayer. I find that honesty builds on honesty, and this brings me closer to the Lord.

I found that one of the biggest hindrances for me was indecision. Sure, I wanted to be honest and not have the urge to lie and deceive all the time, but I'd never taken a conscious *decision* to be honest. In the end it was easy really; all I did was sincerely say to myself and God, *"I now make a decision to be honest. It will not be easy, and I won't get it right straight away, but this is what I want."*

There are many things that pull us away from being honest, but I believe that they all stem from *fear*. We may feel shame and guilt, but even these are essentially rooted in fear – fear of what people might think, say, or do to us. As with everything in this Program, we pray. In order for our fear to go away, we need to change our way of thinking – look at the situation in a different way. We need to see that God is in control. What others think, say or do is not going to hinder the outcome of God's plan for us. If we are destined to be killed there and then, we can rest assured that we will be going home to be with our heavenly Father for eternity. If this happens, it is part of His plan for us, and we have finished what we were put on this earth to do. We may worry about loved ones if we're taken, but God has them in His care – He can look after them just fine without us! If we lose something, including a friendship or favour with others, it may hurt us really badly, but we can be assured that the Lord will be with us at this time.[14] It's nice

---

14. See Matthew 28:20.

to have man's approval, but I can do without it; it's God's approval I really need.

If we can see and understand that who we are in life is not determined by what others think of us or by power and possessions, we can lose a little of that fear already. I personally believe that who we are in this world depends entirely upon our relationship with our Lord God and creator through His Son Jesus Christ. So, if we want to get closer to God, we need to become more honest with Him. God will honour and acknowledge as much as we surrender in honesty.

There is a lot to take in, but we need to grasp this properly. Once we understand the importance of honesty, attaining it is relatively simple. To sum up: we need to make a genuine decision to be honest. Then we need to be as honest as we know how, never neglecting to hand it over to God when we get scared. We must go back and make amends as soon as we are able to do so if we slip up with an untruth. We must just keep this up, no matter what. It is not difficult as long as we don't allow guilt to overcome us; guilt will often be what deters us from pressing on. As we start to be honest little by little, a certain amount of humility creeps into us automatically as we realize how vulnerable we really are. Humility is our next point as we move towards "letting go and letting God".

Humility

A definition of humility is "having or showing a low estimate of one's own importance – of modest pretensions". I found

I achieved a certain amount of humility once I'd become honest to a fault with myself. For the first time in my life, after I truly looked at myself honestly, I saw all the flaws. I saw all the areas where I was not in control at all. I might be the most careful drug user in the world, for example, but somebody could change the drug as I turned my head for a split second, and this could spell the end for me. I could walk out the door the richest and most intelligent man in the world and be killed outright by a speeding car. With this kind of realization, I can humbly admit that I am nothing on my own. This humility naturally resulted from being honest. Can you see how this makes sense?

Once I am humble enough to admit my lack of control over my life, I am more inclined to stop trying to be part of the solution. If I now hand the problem over to God, He is then able to make the change. While I am trying to "help" things along through lies, manipulation, etc., I still do not trust the Lord enough. My humility is therefore only a false humility; I still think I can make a difference to the outcome. I find true humility when I understand that even the talents that I have do not come from my effort in skills development but from the Lord himself. Even the drive and ambition I have is from Him.

And the whole earth was of one language, and of one speech. And it came to pass, as they journeyed from the east, that they found a plain in the land of Shinar; and they dwelt there. And they said one to another, Go to, let us make brick, and burn them thoroughly. And they had brick for stone, and slime had they for morter. And they said, Go to, let us build us a city and a tower, whose top may reach unto heaven; and let us make us a name, lest we be scattered abroad upon the face of the whole earth. And the Lord came down to see the city and the tower, which the children of men builded. And the Lord said, Behold, the people is one, and they have all one language; and this they begin to do: and now nothing will be restrained from them, which they have imagined to do. Go to, let us go down, and there confound their language, that they may not understand one another's speech. So the Lord scattered them abroad from thence upon the face of all the earth: and they left off to build the city. Therefore is the name of it called Babel; because the Lord did there confound the language of all the earth: and from thence did the Lord scatter them abroad upon the face of all the earth. Genesis 11:1-9

This account of the tower of Babel shows who really is in charge ...

I once worked for a very rich boss in construction. He was pretty much what the world would term a "self-made multi-millionaire". He was a hard man and did not seem to care much for others' welfare. He worked hard and put in long hours, and expected it of others, although he never paid accordingly. For instance, he paid the workers for eight hours a day, but would push nine hours out of them. He used to sit with me (I was a site agent, which means I was in charge of an entire construction site) and tell me how he had started at the bottom with one of the big construction companies. After twelve years he had been made a director, which is impressive. Not long after this, he had left that company and started his own company. He told me how he had worked eighteen to nineteen hours a day, how he used to get involved and do the work himself. He said that he had used willpower, determination and self-discipline to get where he was, and I believed him. However, he thought that these qualities were self-made, that the breaks he got in life were of his own working.

Don't get me wrong, I believe he used his skills very well, as did the servant who received ten talents in the Parable of the Talents.[15] However, he seemed unaware of the fact that his skills had been given to him exclusively and that they came from God. He also seemed oblivious to the many gifts he received from God in his daily life; I think he took many things for granted. I don't think he saw self-discipline as a gifting, for instance. I don't believe he understood or saw that his deals falling into place, or the fact that there were no major disasters on his sites, as being actual blessings from God. He gave the impression that all these things had been achieved through his own hard work and careful planning. He said he did believe in God, but I don't think whether he was a Christian or not is relevant to these skills and blessings. The Bible says:

> *Before I formed thee in the belly I knew thee; and before thou camest forth out of the womb I sanctified thee, and I ordained thee a prophet unto the nation.*
>
> Jeremiah 1:5

It also says:

> *That ye may be the children of your Father which is in heaven: for he maketh his sun to rise on the evil and*

---

15. See Matthew 25:14-29.

on the good, and sendeth rain on the just and on the unjust.   Matthew 5:45

These scriptures tell me that God had a plan for us (our free will might have spoilt those plans somewhat), and that what He has intended to give us He still does, irrespective of whether or not we choose to follow Him or even acknowledge Him. So, what we do or don't do has no bearing on what God does or doesn't do for us. Therefore, how can we claim any accolade?

Simply put, this is what I understand humility to be: *I am nothing but an empty vessel without God.* All that I am and will be is because of God and His power and will. His will allowed me to exercise my will, even if it meant deviating from His plan for me. Humility is being conscious and aware of where my power, ability and the circumstances surrounding me come from, and giving God the credit for any praise, accolades and blessings that might be thrown my way. If I claim any credit for anything in my life without first understanding and then accrediting it to God, I am the opposite of humble. For me, humility can be summed up in one phrase: *I can't, but through me, He can.*

In my own experience, I have come to realize that I only have control over one thing in my life, and that is my will. In the past I have chosen to use my free will in all the wrong areas of self-gratification. This was totally selfish. I found that the alcohol, drugs and sex gave me a false sense of well-being. I had chosen this way; I had not been forced into it. The addictions had grabbed a hold of me, though. Once I realized that this was all false I had to let go of all pride, even false pride (*"Look how good I am for letting go"*). God was the master of my destiny, as He had created me. So, I became humble enough to realize that in order to achieve serenity (peace of mind), I had to *choose* to get my will in line with God's will.

The only thing I found that works for me is to hand my free will back to God and ask Him to put it in line with His will for me, and I need to do this daily. This is the active part we play in the process, and it does not always come easily. The battle with self in all aspects of life is an ongoing one. I need to constantly remind myself of the inadequacy I have and hand it over to the Lord. I can then take the "me" out of the picture and when this happens, God is able to ring the changes in me.

I would like to discuss something I like to call "bold humility". This statement might sound paradoxical, but the fact is that we are not exercising boldness because of what we see and believe about ourselves, but rather in the belief and realization of what God can and will do through us if we let Him. This means that we don't have to be anybody's doormat; we stand our ground in a respectful manner, and yet we can humbly apologize for our wrongdoing in whichever situation we may need to. This we achieve by doing a spot inventory (see Step 10).

I can do all things through Christ which strengtheneth me.   Philippians 4:13

When I read this my focus is on the fact that it is Christ's strength and not mine. This keeps me humble, and knowing God as the all-powerful creator and that He is with me, gives me the boldness needed to do whatever needs doing. How awesome is that!

There's been something I have battled my whole life to understand and something I have only recently been able get my head around. And that is I could never understand why some people seemed so lucky and others not. Though truthfully, my mind was probably more focused on why I was so unlucky. This wonder never dissipated when I moved into a real relationship with God, but I found that my focus had shifted off myself and onto others. I believe that my relationship with God was a true act of His grace given to me. What I mentally grappled with was why it had been withheld from me in the first place and then so freely given, why it was not given to some others and why still, some received it so early on in their lives. A while back now I read two books, *What's So Amazing About Grace?* by Philip Yancy[16] and *Humility* by Andrew Murray,[17] and I found the answers to my questions. What I am going to share now is how I understand God to have revealed it to me, and it may be that God reveals it to you differently. The way we understand something should not have any impact on our relationship with God if we are truthful. At the time I was establishing a close relationship with God, I had no understanding of what was going on; I was only desperate to stop drinking (it was busy killing me), and was therefore willing to do the Program as suggested.

The way I understand grace is like this: assistance of any kind that is given without merit, without being earned and with no conditions attached. I had the impression that God's grace was for specific people only, and that the criteria for who would receive it was one of God's mysteries, and that whatever was given to me should be accepted with gratitude. The idea of gratitude and acceptance without question sat well with me, but what I could not get my

16. Philip Yancy, *What's So Amazing About Grace* (Zondervan), ISBN 9780310245650.
17. Andrew Murray, *Humility* (Rickfords Hill Publishing Ltd), ISBN 9781905044405.

head around was that a fair and loving God would reserve His grace for some and not for others. In many aspects, as demonstrated in the parable of the talents, this is the case. Some people are graced with intelligence, skills, natural drive and ambition, etc., while others seem to have none of these attributes. In fact, some end up with hindrances such as learning disabilities, physical disabilities, low drive or unfavourable situations and circumstances. Paul says, however:

> *Actually, I don't have a sense of needing anything personally. I've learned by now to be quite content whatever my circumstances. I'm just as happy with little as with much, with much as with little. I've found the recipe for being happy whether full or hungry, hands full or hands empty. Whatever I have, wherever I am, I can make it through anything in the One who makes me who I am.* Philippians 4:12-13 (MSG)

Paul has the solution: we are to focus on the right thing as our source of joy, which is God. God is able to give us joy in any circumstance because our circumstances are not what make us joyful or not, our relationship with Him does.

The way I have come to understand it is that grace is given to everybody right from the beginning. All we need to do is to accept it, but this is where the problem starts. You need to be humble in order to accept grace with all its blessings. I say this because of the manner in which grace is offered. Grace was given to us, in effect, before we were born. (I say "in effect" as God does not operate within the parameters of time as we do.) Therefore, I cannot do or not do anything to "up" my grace; it was already given to me in full. I am not deserving of it in any way, I cannot love God more to receive a larger portion, and I cannot do anything more in this world for others to improve my stakes; *God has already given it all to me.* He knew what I would do with my free will right from the start, so He knew I was going to need His help, which comes in the form of grace. That is why I believe that in order to accept such a gift, I have to be humble. No one who thinks they have humility, or thinks they are deserving of humility, or believes they have worked hard to achieve humility, is truly humble in my opinion. I say this because I believe true humility stems from a real trust, belief and understanding, that has come through revelation,[18] that everything I am and can be, is because of the power of God in my life and in my circumstances. Because of this, I don't believe anyone who is proud (by this I am meaning not humble) can truly accept the gift of grace, because their very nature cannot accept something so freely offered with "no strings attached". People without true humility will in some way try to reason out a way to believe that there has got to be something within themselves that must have warranted a certain amount of credit, and therefore partially deserving of grace. When this thought is somewhere in the mind, even if it is a sub-conscious thought, we cannot take the grace proffered.[19]

---

18. I believe that revelation is a supernatural understanding that comes to us personally by the Holy Spirit.

19. It is not the person's fault that they can't receive it. I believe the feeling that we need to earn something, and therefore are somehow deserving of that thing, is very much part of our fleshly nature and this is reinforced all the time through secular, and (sadly) sometimes Christian groups as well. Without God's help through the means of revelation from the Holy Spirit, none of us can grasp this properly. A word I hear thrown around a lot in the world today is, *deserving*. "Pete is so deserving of that promotion", or "Ann really shouldn't have come first; she doesn't deserve it." No one is deserving or not deserving of anything; it's all given or not given as is God's pleasure, *"Having predestined us unto the adoption of children by Jesus Christ to himself, according to the good pleasure of his will, To the praise of the glory of his grace, wherein he hath made us accepted in the beloved"* (Ephesians 1:5-6).

Herein lies the big issue; most people feel that they are humble, or that they can become humble if they set their minds to it. However, the minute one says, "I'm going to be humble from now on," the ego is there, because it's all about what *you* are going to do. That is why my understanding of humility is, "I can't, but through me, He can."

In my case, and certainly in working with people with dependency disorders, I have realized we are riddled with pride, ego and self. I could never see that I was like this before the revelation came, even when others filmed me and showed it to me the next day. I always had an excuse which generally centred around the theme that I was "hard done by".

So, to sum up my woes: I was not in relationship with God (and was of all people most miserable), but I could not get into relationship with God without Him helping me. He had already given me help in the form of grace, but I could not access it because my pride, ego and self-centredness made it impossible for me to do so. I needed humility in order to accept His grace and the blessings and miracles that come with it. My unseen problem (self) was the thing blinding me from what I needed in my life (humility), in order to attain the solution (God's grace).

Here is where the miracle of the Program comes in. I heard how others had discovered intimacy in relationship with God and, through the God-given gift of discomfort, I was willing to do exactly what they had said they'd done to establish this relationship with God. There was not much mention of grace and humility and the like. I was told that if I wanted a real relationship with God, I had to simply work through the Program (the steps), and that they would show me how. I needed to be as honest and thorough as I could be (which wasn't very much initially). This is all I knew and understood, so I did the Program that took me about six months, and, without any major fireworks, I became acutely aware that God was there: in me, around me, in my thoughts – doing for me what I could never do for myself. What the Program did for me while I was totally oblivious to even needing it, is that it deflated my ego and pride. I thereby achieved a certain amount of humility, which gave me access to enough of God's grace so that I was able to open the door and step aside as He came in and "supped" with me (Revelation 3:20.) In all my dealings with problems and character defects, the only approach that has brought me victory has been this process.

I came to see as clear as daylight just how full of pride, ego and self I was, and I remember feeling truly ashamed. I still suffer with these things on a daily basis, but the difference is that I can see them now, and this has allowed me to tackle many of my defects of character. The more humility that comes in, the more grace is attainable. After this I could really understand 2 Corinthians 12:9:

> And he said unto me, My grace is sufficient for thee: for my strength is made perfect in weakness. Most gladly therefore will I rather glory in my infirmities, that the power of Christ may rest upon me.

Paul realized that the more he accepted his powerlessness, the more of God's grace was available to help him.

I often felt empathy for people who seemed less fortunate than me. This is not in itself a bad thing, but I once sat in an old, retired pastor's "humble abode" and listened as he and his wife shared some of their lives with me. He had nothing, his health was deteriorating rapidly, he had children and grandchildren following their own paths and who really "sponged" what they could off his meagre pension. Yet he had something that I wanted so badly; an incredible love and relationship with God that brings a lump to my throat even as I sit here and write. He never spoke about the problems around him, only about the wonderful things the Lord had done for him in his life. As he spoke of these things, tears of absolute gratitude and love would choke him up and his wife would have to continue with the story. I knew that this old man had more than I could ever dream of having, he had received a large amount of God's grace that was available to him.

We often feel we were given a raw deal when God's "talents" were dished out to us, when actually we have just been focused the whole time on things that are not important; things that do not bring us peace, joy and contentment in a close relationship with Him. I am starting to understand why Jesus said:

> But seek ye first the kingdom of God, and his righteousness; and all these things shall be added unto you.   Matthew 6:33

Humility, although explained in a simple way, is a task that is not easy for us. Self is always rearing up. Humility does not come easily, so we need to keep it in our daily prayers. Our Lord God is the creator and is all-powerful. We need to ask Him daily for His help and guidance.

This understanding brings us to the final point in the move towards "letting go and letting God": perseverance.

Karin's Story

It is now almost ten years ago that by the grace of God, I finally said goodbye to what I believed to have been my two best friends: drugs and alcohol.

My story is a whirlwind of personal hurt, then addiction, lies and destruction. Losing my father in a way I could not understand led me to rebel. This, mixed with bad influences and poor choices, meant that I lost myself, others, and everything I held dear to me.

It is at this point that I would like to thank my parents for a good upbringing. It is because of their upbringing that even at my lowest point, I always respected my body. Thank you, Mamsie and Pappie!

By God's grace (you will find I say this a lot!), I met someone at a random party. He was different from others I had met, and I sometimes find myself wondering whether he would have come and introduced himself that night had he known then what he knows now. He is now my husband of six years, in which I have been sober the whole time. My Ian! After everything I put him through, by God's grace, he has stuck by me and has never left me. Through the Lord's intervention, Ian found it in his heart to forgive me wholeheartedly and to trust me again once I became sober. I believe that this has helped me in renewing and growing my faith and trust in God.

Now, back to my story. I was in and out of rehabs, and it was Ian who arranged all of this. In fact, there was so much help offered to me, a very dear friend even helped with funds (praise God that he is still my friend today), family members opened their homes to me in loving attempts to help me, and today I want to thank them from the bottom of my heart, even though I messed it up each and every time.

I eventually ended up at my sister and her husband's place, Petra and Francois. At this stage I had literally lost everything. Even Ian had to remove himself from the situation (he was always in the background though, making sure I was ok). I cringe at the thought of how tough this must have been for Petra and Francois, opening their home, and having to witness my self-destruction daily. Anika, my oldest sister, never lived close by, but for a very long time she helped and supported me, including financially. But I was so lost; I was finished! I must give honour to both my sisters for trying their best to help me throughout my journey.

A very good friend Issi and her husband were very supportive of me and many was the night that I crashed (passed out) on their couch after being on a bender. At some point they too needed to withdraw themselves from helping me and actually, I was partly grateful for this, as I was in no state to be a friend to them – I felt I had become a terrible human being. (Years after I had recovered, by God's grace, Issi found it in her heart to forgive me, and Ian and I even attended their wedding – thank You, Lord.)

I remember the night when Issi took me to my first Christian-based Program meeting. This is where I met Pauline and Rory, and they played a crucial part in my recovery, as each of them mentored myself and Ian, with Rory being a mentor to me, and Pauline to Ian separately.

(Yes, even after we split up, Ian attended the meetings with me.) The thing that was different with these meetings compared to all the other previous institutes and meetings I attended, was that there was a "light" present in others, a light that I wanted to experience for myself. I have now found this light, which was the light of Jesus all along. I could relate in so many ways to what was shared, and for the first time in my life I really wanted to be better, even though I still continued to mess up.

It was the afternoon of 18th July 2013 when I was still living with my sister and her husband; I had just lost my last work opportunity by arriving drunk and humiliating myself at work. I left Liezl (my boss at the time and dear friend today) without any explanation. I really had nothing left. I remember that Petra and Francois were going away for the weekend, and Francois, who had become fed up, asked me to please not break the house down. I was alone: no money, no friends, no transport, and no drugs or alcohol . . .

I remember it like it was yesterday. I was sitting in the lounge feeling so sorry for myself, fighting a terrible come down. It was then in my lowest ebb that I truly called upon the Lord for the first time: *"Lord, I am begging You for help. I have no power over this addiction. But Lord, I know that You have. I surrender completely. Please take control of my body and my mind. I have nothing to offer You, but I promise I will not be ashamed to tell people that You are alive. I will live my life daily to tell people that You saved my life. No one else can help me, Lord; only You can through Jesus Christ who died for my sins. Lord, I am sorry that they are really bad sins . . ."*

I fell asleep and awoke the next day with no cravings and no withdrawal symptoms. A few days passed, and I was still sober. I remember just putting my focus on the Lord; taking it one day at a time.

About a week later I phoned Liezl. By God's grace she answered my call, even though she had no reason to. Before I could say a word, she said, "See you tomorrow" – I mean . . . what? I went back to work the next day and Liezl smiled when she saw me. Throughout the day she treated and loved me as if nothing had happened; she forgave me wholeheartedly. I am grateful to still have Liezl as a dear friend today.

This part of the story marks the start of my road of recovery, working the Program, but with my focus on God. Making amends was a big part of it and I found it was the breakthrough I needed. God gave me the strength to make amends to Ian, my sisters, my family, friends and others I'd harmed. Some will never forgive me, but God gave me the strength to accept that. God also helps me daily to deal with the guilt and regret, and trust me when I say, there is a lot!

When I did this Program, all I was looking for was to stay sober and live a normal life, but something happened that I never bargained for. Yes, I am sober and living a normal life, but the true miracle is that I find myself in a deep and personal relationship with God, through the Holy Spirit and Jesus. I find He is with me; I talk to Him and get a real sense of comfort and peace. I had been a Christian before, but I had never experienced this. It was not a big "flashy" thing that happened; it almost seemed as if, quite out of the blue, God was there – next to me, in me, with me. I know

I am weak and yet I seem to have this power and ability to do things that I hand over to Him. This is what has been missing in my soul, and I am so surprised at how doing this Program has brought this about; it's truly a miracle.

I think what I am trying to focus on with my story is that I had no control over my life. I knew about Jesus, but I chose to not live my life according to His Word. He saved my life, and I am not just talking about my addiction. By accepting Jesus Christ as my Saviour, I can live my life sober. Every day has meaning. I want to be a better person, and this *will* is something I know God has placed in me. By asking for forgiveness when I do wrong, I want to learn from my mistakes, and I have the desire to live a life that will make Him proud.

The power of prayer is something I can go on about for a long time. I see it daily; I am alive because of it, and I often wonder how a happy life can be lived without Jesus. With Him in my life now, every single challenge I face, I never have to deal with it on my own again. Will I get hurt? Yes. Will there be times of sadness and disappointment? Yes. Will things happen that I will never understand? Of course. I am human, living in a world of sin and I have the "fleshly" life to contend with. I still sin daily, even though I don't want to, but knowing that Jesus died for my *every* sin makes me want to be a better human every day. I want to make Him a proud Father, and one day I will understand everything, including my father's (and now mother's) passing. For now, I am so grateful to know both of them are with our Father in heaven, and they are pain free; that is enough for me.

And then there is grace . . . there is always grace. I live by grace. God's grace saved me. Every person I met along the way, every hard and good lesson I have learned, every unique human created by God that I might help with my little story – even just with a smile, a kind word or a prayer – this is His grace given, as I realize I have been given another life. Saved by the grace of Jesus Christ. I know that this grace was always freely available to me. However, it was only once I had completed the work in the Program, that it seemed I was able to truly accept this grace that had been there on offer all the time. I am able to accept it just as I am, not because I deserve it, but because I am chosen and loved by God – just as I am.

I would like to end with a one liner that a dear friend in my "new life" said to me when I was having a tough day (and those tough days will still come): *"When God looks at you, He sees perfection."* Mind blowing, right?! That is enough for me. Jesus is enough . . . by His grace.

Perseverance

A definition of perseverance is "steadfast pursuit of an aim, constant persistence; continuance in a state of grace". I know that developing an intimate relationship with God is a journey and not a destiny, therefore I am going to need perseverance and God's grace to be allowed to make mistakes and yet continue. I think the key here for me was to recognize that this continuance is "in a state of grace". Without this grace, we would have been doomed no matter what. This is what God has granted us through the death of His Son Jesus Christ, and for which I am eternally grateful. I need to show gratitude for this by thanking God daily and by passing this message on to others, which is part of His will for my life and a vital part of my relationship with the Lord.

Many words and actions are closely linked to perseverance: patience, tolerance, long-suffering, self-control, forgiveness, endurance, stamina, courage and focus. A lot of these are the fruits of the Spirit.[20] Perseverance is needed to acquire most of the tools we need in our walk with God. Once we're convinced that this is the course of action we need to take, we can make a choice to do so with the comfort that it will be a journey until we leave this world – one we do not take alone, but with the Holy Spirit to guide us and our sponsors (mentors) and the Program to support us. We have another guarantee in God's Word that tells us to rejoice in hard times, as it's not always a bad thing or a punishment to go through problems and trials.

And not only so, but we glory in tribulations also: knowing that tribulation worketh patience; And patience, experience; and experience, hope: And hope maketh not ashamed; because the love of God is shed abroad in our hearts by the Holy Ghost which is given unto us. Romans 5:3-5

Strength of character is what we need to overcome our defects of character. If you are showing strength of character in an area of your life, you won't be defective of character in that area, will you? God tells us that we will not be shamed when we hope, and this is what really gives me courage to persevere when it's tough!

20. See Galatians 5:22-23.

I believe that perseverance lost its value in the world with the fast pace of technology and a world promoting instant gratification. Some young people became multi-millionaires in the space of a year or two with their computers and the Internet. Programmers and web designers in their teens were leaving school and going into a market which lacked trained computer "people". The efficiency of computers and the Internet in business warranted quick change at any cost. The slogan "time is money" rang true and was pushed to the limit. "Takeaway food" became known as "fast food", with some restaurants even boasting that the food purchased would be given free if not delivered on time! What about life? Nobody wants to do the "horrible" bits of life; we try to ignore them, bypass them or speed through them. Why cook when you can get nutritious pre-cooked meals? One saves on time, money and cleaning up all that mess after cooking.

The character defects that arise in our lives, some of which are directly derived from the lack of proper social interaction caused by everything being sped up, are treated with the same "fast food" attitude as the rest of our lives. Go and see a psychiatrist and get on some medication for the lack of energy, insomnia, irritable bowel syndrome, depression, anxiety, frustration, anger – I could increase the list ad infinitum. Please note, however, that I am not downing psychiatry or the use of medication in any way; they do have their place. What I am saying is that whilst some of our defective character traits have been learned over a considerable period of time, often as subconscious defensive or coping mechanisms, in other cases the root cause is simple self-centredness – self-will out of control, sometimes due to a lack of adequate discipline and boundaries during childhood.

Whatever the reason, it all boils down to this: the inability to see anything through to the end. *If it doesn't work quickly, bin it and try something else.* The hard truth is that there is no quick fix. It took many years to build up these defects, and it is going to take many years to be free of them. Added to this, we need to realize that this job is our responsibility. We need to take responsibility for our own character defects and dependencies, even though we do not necessarily need to take the blame for having them. The real good news is that we do not need to do it alone. We have the Lord God who is there to assist and comfort us, and the Program and our sponsors for support. We need to make a decision to follow a plan and see it through no matter what!

I have already touched a bit on what I believe the world's view of a quick fix is; let's see what the Lord has to say . . .

The Pharisees also with the Sadducees came, and tempting desired him that he would shew them a sign from heaven. He answered and said unto them, When it is evening, ye say, It will be fair weather: for the sky is red. And in the morning, It will be foul weather to day: for the sky is red and lowering. O ye hypocrites, ye can discern the face of the sky; but can ye not discern the signs of the times? A wicked and adulterous generation seeketh after a sign; and there shall no sign be given unto it, but the sign of the prophet Jonas. And he left them, and departed. Matthew 16:1-4

The Pharisees wanted a sign as proof that Jesus was the Messiah, and we do the same when we expect an instant deliverance or miracle from God. I'm not saying it doesn't

85

happen, in fact I am living proof that it does. The point here is that the expectation of a quick fix is the one sure way to set ourselves up for a slip or a fall. It takes a lifetime of focus to remain in true relationship with God.

Even though I experienced the instant miracle deliverance from my discomfort that a lot of us look for, I was only aware of this after three months or so into the process.

I cannot begin to fathom God's way of doing things. I recommend reading chapters 38 to 41 in the Book of Job, which helped understand this. Here is just one part:

Then the Lord answered Job out of the whirlwind, and said, Who is this that darkeneth counsel by words without knowledge? Gird up now thy loins like a man; for I will demand of thee, and answer thou me. Where wast thou when I laid the foundations of the earth? declare, if thou hast understanding. Who hath laid the measures thereof, if thou knowest? or who hath stretched the line upon it? Whereupon are the foundations thereof fastened? or who laid the corner stone thereof; When the morning stars sang together, and all the sons of God shouted for joy? Job 38:1-7

With this in mind, how can I have any *expectations* of how, when, where and for how long God will work in my life and relationship with Him? And since I've established that I am dealing with character defects that were formed over a period of at least thirty-three years of my life, I now know that there will be no ultimate quick fix. We will need to persevere through the tough times. When we recognize this truth, we are less likely to be disappointed by the difficulties in the process and more aware of the small victories God gives us along the way. I can trust God, even if nothing materializes for me here on earth. Jeremiah – also known as the weeping prophet – was a major prophet who spoke to the people of Judah under God's instruction on many occasions, and they never listened to him. *"What a waste!"* we might say. Not so in God's eyes. You see, it's the perseverance in the face of adversity that pleases God. Jeremiah is one of God's most beloved in heaven. We see from the story of Job that God later blessed him with double what he had, and he lived a long life:

And the Lord turned the captivity of Job, when he prayed for his friends: also the Lord gave Job twice as much as he had before. Then came there unto him all his brethren, and all his sisters, and all they that had been of his acquaintance before, and did eat bread with him in his house: and they bemoaned him, and comforted him over all the evil that the Lord had brought upon him: every man also gave him a piece of money, and every one an earring of gold. So the Lord blessed the latter end of Job more than his beginning: for he had fourteen thousand sheep, and six thousand camels, and a thousand yoke of oxen, and a thousand she asses. He had also seven sons and three daughters. And he called the name of the first, Jemima; and the name of the second, Kezia; and the name of the third, Kerenhappuch. And in all the land were no women found so fair as the daughters of Job: and their father gave them inheritance among their brethren. After this lived Job an hundred and forty years, and saw his sons, and his sons' sons, even four generations.

Job 42:10-16

I believe everybody should have a special scripture or verse from the Bible that either inspires them or lifts them up. One of mine is:

The steps of a good man are ordered by the Lord: and he delighteth in his way. Though he fall, he shall not be utterly cast down: for the Lord upholdeth him with his hand. Psalm 37:23-24

The reason that it appeals to me so much is that it is so realistic with regard to everyday life. The best aspect of this verse is that it teaches He delights in *our* ways. God loves me, period.

I have a son and when he was little, he'd get up to real mischief. When I caught him, he'd look so innocent, as if butter wouldn't melt in his mouth. It was in times like these that I felt my heart melt for him, and I'd love him to bits. It brought me immense joy. My dad had the same experience with me when I was three years old. He needed to fit the sprinkler head to the garden hose and said I should turn the tap on when he called and said he was done. Apparently, I peered around the corner of the house and saw he was still busy, then proceeded to turn the tap on full. My father was drenched, and I ran away laughing my head off. When my dad tells this story, he does so with fond memories of deep love. This is what I feel God sees in me too. He knows that I'm His child and that I want to do the right things, but sometimes in my eagerness, I mess it up. I believe He loves us all the more and it brings great delight to Him. The Lord is also saying here that we are on a journey (the steps), which will require us to persevere; all journeys do. It then tells us that we are human and fallible ("Though he fall . . ."), which I need to never forget – I've tried it my way and made a right mess of everything in my life. But I can persevere with confidence and not futility because I have God's assurance that I will be held up by Him so that I can continue the journey.

There's an old saying in sporting circles: *"It isn't losing to get knocked down; losing is staying down."* We're not going to "win 'em all", but that isn't the bigger picture. We learn and grow and gain experience by defeats. But are they really defeats when they are providing so much more for us in the long run? I used to play a lot of chess at school and one of my favourite plays was the Gambit. This is when you sacrifice a piece for a far better strategic position or ultimate gain. Many times this led to winning the game. We have such an advantage as children of God because we have this promise from above and can be assured that defeats are all part of the plan to overcome our defects.

Count it all joy, my brothers, when you meet trials of various kinds, for you know that the testing of your faith produces steadfastness. And let steadfastness have its full effect, that you may be perfect and complete, lacking in nothing. James 1:2-4 (ESV)

I have reached a point in my life where I have realized that since I have given my life over to God, it is His job to look after me, and I know He can. Even if I doubted that He could take care of me, I can take strength in the fact that I know that I cannot (I've already proved that to myself many times), and therefore anything that He can do for me is far better than what I had before. This way of thinking allows me to persevere even if a battle seems lost. It's a journey and way of life; I can't lose as long as I don't give up.

I love getting instructions from the Lord; not because they're easy but because I know then that I am on the right track. Over and above this, obedience is the best demonstration of love, and I want to show God my love.

Patient endurance is what you need now, so that you will continue to do God's will. Then you will receive all that he has promised. Hebrews 10:36 (NLT)

We give great honour to those who endure under suffering. For instance, you know about Job, a man of great endurance. You can see how the Lord was kind to him at the end, for the Lord is full of tenderness and mercy. James 5:11 (NLT)

How wonderful! We are even given a promise of reward in the end. However, I have found through my experience that it is not good for me to keep this promise of reward as my motivation to be patient and endure. I find that I rob myself if I do this. The greatest fulfilment I've found I get is when I do these things for God because I want to – for free. This is love, and it pleases God. The apostle Simon Peter explains the process beautifully:

In view of all this, make every effort to respond to God's promises. Supplement your faith with a generous provision of moral excellence, and moral excellence with knowledge, and knowledge with self-control, and self-control with patient endurance, and patient endurance with godliness, and godliness with brotherly affection, and brotherly affection with love for everyone. The more you grow like this, the more productive and useful you will be in your knowledge of our Lord Jesus Christ. 2 Peter 1:5-8 (NLT)

This is the work God wants us to persevere with; it is His job to look after us and take care of our problematic lives and struggles. While we are persevering with our instructions to help others, knowing that God is there to uphold and guide us, and we're not interfering with His job of trying to "fix" us, He takes care of our affairs. This is what it's all about. The Lord of heaven gave us free will and freedom of choice. We chose to give our will back to Him and to hand Him control of our lives, and to persevere through hardships as we do His will. Jesus Christ has told us what God's will is:

A new commandment I give unto you, That ye love one another; as I have loved you, that ye also love one another. John 13:34

I have read about, and heard many godly people speak on this, and I have tried many different ways to love. In my experience, the best way that we can love someone is to do things for them that they need done, and to do these things because we want to, for free and for the enjoyment.

Nothing in the world can take the place of persistence (perseverance). Talent will not; nothing is more common than unsuccessful men with talent. Genius will not; unrewarded genius is almost a proverb. Education will not; the world is filled with educated derelicts. Persistence and determination are alone omnipotent. "Press on!" has been and always will be the answer to every human problem.[21] Calvin Coolidge

---

21. www.goodreads.com/quotes/2749-nothing-in-this-world-can-take-the-place-of-persistence

I believe this to be true, provided we are in God's will. Nelson Mandela was imprisoned for twenty-seven years. He could have forgotten everything and rotted away, but instead he studied and became a lawyer, and he wrote books which have inspired a nation and, indeed, the world. He came out of prison and became president of South Africa, and a world icon of peaceful transformation and democracy. You see, it's easy to become discouraged in the face of adversity and not to persevere when obstacles line our journey, but we are privileged to have a loving Father God to be with us. We have our groups and sponsors (someone whom we can call for any help, who is in the Program – the journey) to encourage us. Being in a Program and having a sponsor has been vital in my journey and is quite biblical.

Confess your faults one to another, and pray one for another, that ye may be healed. The effectual fervent prayer of a righteous man availeth much. James 5:16

This healing is also internal healing from discouragement, fatigue and disillusionment.

We are on a new journey into a deep relationship with God. It is ongoing and it has its disappointments and what feels like setbacks. Once we understand that this is normal and that we will have tough times, we can set our minds to the task of persevering. I have found that this simple formula works for me, and when it doesn't work, I just keep doing it, no matter what, until I am through the crisis or trial:

- I pray and ask God to take my problem and deal with it because I can't.

- I do a personal inventory (Step 10) and make restitution where I see I've gone wrong.

- I pick up the phone and call a sponsor/friend and go for coffee, or just talk to them. I tell them my situation and ask them to pray for me.

- I pray for an opportunity and look out for anyone I can assist or help with whatever they may need – for free and for pleasure.

- I praise and thank God for the many good things He's done in my life and for all the blessings He has given me (there are many if you just think about it and ask the Lord to reveal them to you).

Usually, at this point I feel good and can move on. But if not, I simply repeat this formula over and over again; if nothing else, I feel peace and inner joy while doing this.

I follow this pattern continually as part of doing God's work, but when trials or adversities come along, I do these things with greater intensity and with greater awareness.

Our greatest strength lies in the knowledge that without God we have no strength. I know this because the Bible says:

In him we live, and move, and have our being.

Acts 17:28

Amen!

The Simplicity of the Process

Just do it

For me the simplicity of the Program came in when I realized how utterly powerless I was. No matter what I tried to do I still felt empty and distanced from God. I believe this fact alone was my saving grace. In most other areas of my life, with enough willpower and determination, I was able to attain a reasonable semblance of normality, or so I thought. For years I tried to get the Holy Spirit in me so that I could feel some kind of connection with God, and these attempts were sincere, as I'm sure many of you can relate to if you have felt the same. I was mainly fear-driven because of where I saw my life headed, but eventually even the fear of where I was going to end up left me, and only the hopelessness remained.

It was in this state that I spoke to God with complete abandon and asked Him for His help. I had already done Step 1 – I'd admitted that I was powerless, and that my life was unmanageable. I had also done Step 3 – I'd decided to turn my will and my life over to the care of God, as I understood Him. Because I had grown up in a Christian home, the only God I had understood was the Lord God of heaven and earth through His Son Jesus Christ. However, I did not fully believe that He could restore me to sanity or that I was really insane for that matter, so my Step 2 was incomplete at this stage. I did manage to hand the problem over to God, which suggests a measure of belief, even though I think it was mainly because of my desperation that I did hand it over.

I had no faith. I had done the action (Step 3) without the belief (Step 2). In Exodus 14:15-22 and Joshua 3:5-16, both Moses and Joshua had to take the action before the miracle happened. Moses raised his staff and *then* the waters of the Red Sea parted. As the Levite priests under Joshua's orders touched the waters of the Jordan River, the river dried up at this place. Moses and Joshua had enough belief to take the action, and this is essentially all it takes.

This is how I made the true connection with the Lord. It was as simple and miraculous as that! In fact, it was so simple and subtle that it was a few months before I realized that God was already doing for me what I could not do for myself. It was then that I completed my Step 2, as I came to realize that God had restored me to sanity, and the miracle was complete.

Now, I am not under any illusion in thinking that it comes this quickly to all people, or with all the different issues we face in life. Since then, I have tried to tackle other defects of character in the same way; that is, I have tried to practise these principles in all my affairs (Step 12), and it hasn't been as easy. However, all is not lost. I have overcome many of these character defects and I am still busy with others, with many to come as the Lord reveals them to me. I use the exact same system of asking for his help with complete abandon.

The added factor now needed I've found, is *perseverance.*[22] I realize that we have already discussed perseverance earlier, but I would like to touch on it a bit more here, as I believe that grasping this is extremely important to the process. Perseverance is to endure hardships with patience and steadfastness, in spite of opposition or discouragement, and in the face of obstacles during an undertaking. I believe that this is where the battle rages hardest in us. There is a wonderful scripture in which Jesus says:

> But I tell you this – though he won't do it for friendship's sake, if you keep knocking long enough, he will get up and give you whatever you need because of your shameless persistence. And so I tell you, keep on asking, and you will receive what you ask for. Keep on seeking, and you will find. Keep on knocking, and the door will be opened to you. For everyone who asks, receives. Everyone who seeks, finds. And to everyone who knocks, the door will be opened.
>
> Luke 11:8-10 (NLT)

The key words here are "keep on asking".

So, the message is clear: if what we're are asking help with doesn't come right straight away, we just keep at it. In Luke 9:23 we are instructed to turn from our selfish ways and take up our cross daily and follow Him. For me, the emphasis is on "daily". As I've mentioned before, this suggests a journey rather than a destination. It is the very thought of persistence and struggle that puts most people off. They have often in the past tried some recommended

---

22. See page 82.

solution and become despondent through the lack of results; I know I had!

So how do we motivate ourselves? I found the most amazing thing was that once I'd made the decision and had actually handed it over to God, a subtle, small amount of hope and anticipation crept in on its own. When I felt this, I grabbed onto it with both hands and thanked God for it.

All things come from our heavenly Father, so whatever we lack, He is the perfect person to ask it from. Obviously, it must be in His will for us, but I sincerely believe that asking to have a sincere and intimate relationship with Him, along with all the aspects needed in achieving it, are in His will for us.[23]

Therefore, should I lack motivation for instance, I go down on my knees and ask for motivation every single morning. I simply say something like, "Lord, you know my heart wants to be motivated to follow this suggested process, but I cannot generate the strength to follow it myself. Without your help, Lord, I know that it is impossible to become motivated. So, I am giving this struggle I have to You, and I ask that You will do it for me. Be with me I ask, in Jesus' name. Amen."

I make a decision in my mind to ask the Lord for this every day, regardless of how I feel or what results I see or don't see. This, I believe, is part of what it means to "take up my cross daily".[24]

This is all that is required of me.

---

23. See Luke 11:10.
24. See Luke 9:23.

When I started to do it like this in my life, my way of thinking started to change as well. I found that as my way of thinking changed, so too did my attitude towards the problem. It is then that I found the problem went away. But just like Shadrach, Meshach and Abednego said in the Book of Daniel, I need to make a stand:

If it be so, our God whom we serve is able to deliver us from the burning fiery furnace, and he will deliver us out of thine hand, O king. But if not, be it known unto thee, O king, that we will not serve thy gods, nor worship the golden image which thou hast set up.

Daniel 3:17-18

I had made the decision to rely on God fully, and this scripture gave me the strength to stick at it no matter what. This passage of scripture is one of my favourites and always gives me goosebumps! It stirs such passion in me for the Lord. You see, these three men had thrown their lot in with God. I believe that they had clearly seen the folly of following any other way but the Lord's. The other methods had been tried and tested and had failed. They never fully understood all God's methods but were going to stand by Him no matter what.

I had tried my own way for many years and had failed. I had heard and seen how others had found a true relationship with the Lord, and I was therefore going to stick with that plan no matter what. But just like Shadrach, Meshach and Abednego, I found that the outcome wasn't as bad as it could have been. In my perseverance, I found a quiet peace and comfort that allowed me to continue. This I came to know as serenity. So, whether I was getting it right or not, the fact that I could hand it over to God *each* day made me feel better about myself, rather than if I were not doing that little bit every morning. This part of the experience is just amazing and inexplicable. It is *that simple!*

I don't let guilt at failure get me down because I know it's not my part of the fight; I know I am doing all that is required of me. If the guilt does want to eat at me, I hand it to God with exactly the same prayer; it's truly amazing how it works!

To sum up the simplicity of the Program:

- I have met with absolute defeat and have no hope or faith.

- I tell God honestly of my helplessness, I sincerely hand everything over to Him in prayer, and keep on asking for His help daily, no matter what happens or how I feel.

The Lord God is all powerful and He is able to remove your defects of character, as long as your heart is right! Our life and circumstances are what they are. I believe that if we truly knew the life and relationship God has intended for us in eternity, we'd understand and fully accept our situation. There is a plan for us, and I believe that often our circumstances are part of what is needed to mould us into this plan. I believe that the root of our sinful nature is self. We don't stand a chance in overcoming anything on our own, or successfully achieving anything that God has not preordained for us to achieve. God is our creator, and He always knows how to fix our defects and restore us to His original design. The Program is one of lowering our ego and asking God to come in and do the work. It is by no means easy because our natures fight the yielding process – but it is simple.

PART TWO

The Steps

The Importance of the Process

Nothing is more important to achieving victory in your life than working through the steps of the Program, which is essentially the bulk of the process. Yes, there will be things that you need to do in order to maintain your victory, but I believe that nothing effective will be achieved if you choose not to follow these steps. To start with, you will read through what is written about each step and I am praying and trusting that you will be able to relate to what is written. You will then come to the *action* part of the step, where as you are working through it, you can always refer back to what is written before the *action* part, and I believe this will help you immensely. It's like having a mentor or a second opinion.

Remember, though, that whilst our stories may differ, the most important thing is to see what aspects you can identify with or relate to. I will be sharing what I have learned through other literature and have put into practice, as well as lessons learned through my own experiences that I believe have been fundamental in my journey. Do not become disheartened if you feel that some of the suggestions will just not be possible for you to do. I believe that if your heart is sincere and your motive pure, God will give you the strength that is needed. Also bear in mind that nothing is cast in stone, that God may lead you on a slightly different path. The key here is to be willing to do anything it takes.

Being an alcoholic, I am using the *Twelve Steps*. These steps were originally laid out by the founding members of the organization Alcoholics Anonymous. I have included scripture readings from the Bible that over the years have made sense to me during my quiet times with God. These originate from the organization Alcoholics Victorious.

The fact that we lack power to move into a sincere and intimate relationship with God is probably the reason we are here at this point. We may find this surprising, as we may have been able to achieve a semblance of power in other areas of our lives and maintain it. But as we remained aloof from a real relationship with God, so we may have started to see the "power" sap from these areas of our lives as well. In my case this brought on fear, which in turn brought on desperation as I saw all my best-efforts collapse – unsuccessful and therefore in vain. It was this desperation that made me willing to do this work; it was through God's grace that I found the Program.

We are powerless over everything in our lives except our will and freedom to choose. It is the key to our recovery to get a full understanding of this concept. We need to recognize that up to this point in our lives, we have used this freedom to choose based on our own wants and desires. Remember that this includes good things we have done, but which were actually done to further our own agenda or satisfy some need within us. In short, we have been extremely selfish. This is what I believe has blocked us from God's power, why nothing seemed to happen when we cried out in pain with all the sincerity we could muster. I know I was genuinely sincere.

What we need to do is get rid of *self*. My problem has always been selfishness, ego and pride. The problem is that it is impossible for me to consciously rid myself of these defects. First of all, I could never see my selfishness; I don't believe a selfish person ever can. I always felt I was being hard-done-by and therefore had to take and fight for everything I had and wanted. The second problem was that when I finally recognized my selfish egotistical pride, I couldn't be rid of it.

I recommend trying the following experiment. Make up your mind to be humble and selfless for a day, remembering that real selflessness has no agenda of its own. If you are like me, you will find that it is impossible. The minute I think I'm humble, I've lost my humility in that instant.

I believe that the reason I work through these steps is to remove *myself* from the equation, so that God is able to step in and do the work in my life that I've been asking Him to do all along. God is unable to interfere with our free will, so we need to find a way of humbling ourselves, before He can lift us up.[25] The only way I have found to be humble, is to remove myself from the picture. I had to find a new agenda that did not involve my agenda. Throughout my sobriety, the only thing that has worked for me was to *work through these steps* as willingly, honestly and as open-mindedly as I could.

25. See James 4:10.

My final suggestion is that you do not try to rush through this. It took me the better part of ten months to properly complete the Program, and even then, the final three steps are a basis for our new way of living. So, take your time and let God dictate the pace while you try to enjoy the journey.

Step 1

We admitted we were powerless
over ourselves, that our lives had
become unmanageable.

(Admission)

*For I know that in me (that is, in my flesh,) dwelleth no
good thing: for to will is present with me; but how to
perform that which is good I find not.*   Romans 7:18

What a step! For the first time in my life, I was going to
have to admit that I was powerless over something, and
that basically I could not manage my own life. I had been
taught throughout school and other institutions to never
admit defeat; I'm quite sure you can relate to this.

You might still be at an early stage of your walk with God
and not think there is anything wrong, and that actually,
apart from a few areas of your life, most things you can
handle just fine. The first tell-tale sign is that feeling
of discomfort and uneasiness; that there is something
missing. As the Bible says:

He that hath an ear, let him hear . . .   Revelation 2:7

I certainly didn't hear because, quite frankly, I did not want to listen. I suspect many Christians will not heed this as a sign – I never did – but I have put it in anyway because I believe the grace of God can touch anyone. I still think pain is our best teacher.

I believe that subconsciously we know that there is a problem when we don't sense the Lord's presence in our personal capacity. The big issue we face in admitting defeat is that if the so-called "solution" does not work, we are left "high and dry" – exposed. This is, of course, all our own perception. We have nothing to lose in trying, and everything to gain. We cannot fall further out of relationship with God than we already are, so why do we get the feeling of exposure? There are a lot more Christians out there that are feeling as we do, and they too, are afraid to say so. I believe our open admittance of a lack of true intimacy with God may really help others come out and admit the truth themselves, as they realize that they are not alone. I have found this to be true in most of the times I have spoken about my powerlessness and the unmanageability of my life to others.

If I look back at the unmanageability of my life, I can sum it up quite simply. My life was unmanageable when I could not do the good things that I set my mind to doing. These included responsibilities like commitments, appointments, exercising, taking the dog for a walk, bill payments, housework, servicing the car, being on time for work, etc. I cannot mention any spiritual plans because there weren't any; I was functioning on self-will.

Still, many people battle to get this first step done because they *just don't want to*. I was like that, I wanted God to help me in achieving *my* goals if He would; I was certainly not concerned with what the Lord may have planned for me. The strange thing, though, is that if someone spoke of being in God's will, I would have been the first to say that that was what I was striving for.

I wanted to be able to manage the things in my life that I realized needed managing, without any effort and time. I would mentally commit to paying a bill, visiting my mum, taking my girlfriend to the movies, going to a function or whatever. The evening before, I'd go for a drink after work and get home at 3am, and so I would end up missing my commitment. I could not manage my life.

That was a description of my drinking life, and I thought that once I had found freedom from alcohol that managing my life would be automatic and easy. Not so; the powerlessness I now had went something like this:

I wake up on Monday morning and spend time praying, meditating and reading my Bible. I know that I battle with a bit of road rage as well as colourful language, and so I ask the Lord to help me to be patient, calm and to keep my bad language in check. I also know that the Word says that today is the day that the Lord has made, and we are to rejoice and be glad in it,[26] so I tell God that this is what I will do. I also tell Him that I will look for someone to help and just help them, no strings attached. After praying this, I feel really good inside and am ready to face the day, knowing that I am on a good footing for the day, and that the Lord will be with me and will be really pleased with me.

---

26. See Psalm 118:24.

I get into my car and set off to work. I haven't been in the traffic long before someone comes flying out of nowhere and pushes in front of me, forcing me to slam on my brakes to avoid going into the back of them. I hoot and flash my lights, shouting in "French" at them; silly really, as of course they cannot hear me. I drive on, playing the scenario over and over in my mind. I keep wondering to myself what would have happened if I hadn't seen them. I wonder still, if I'd had my wife or one of my grandchildren in the car and they had been injured . . . I get even more upset by this, and I feel perfectly justified in my reaction. I hope my reaction would be enough to deter the person from doing something so dangerous again. The problem now is that I am not rejoicing in the day, and I am still upset and on edge. I get to work at the same time as someone else and I pull right into a parking space that they were also going for. I can feel a little niggle and un-comfortability in the pit of my stomach the whole day. I have a really miserable day and that night, as I take a bath and reflect over things, it all comes back to me.

Why do I do this? Why can't I just let the other driver be, and thank the Lord He was there to prevent an accident? After all, I'd prayed and "decided" most sincerely this morning about it all . . . Why do I keep using bad language? Why can't I stop and just use more civil words? All other Christians can . . . Where was my rejoicing in this day? I hardly spent ten minutes in the world rejoicing . . . What happened to helping someone else? I totally missed the opportunity to help someone by shooting into the parking space before the other person could, just because I got there first . . . I so wanted to have done something nice for someone else . . . Can you see, *I am powerless!*

This description of the type of things I deal with might be heavier or milder than the scenarios you may face in your life, but the question is the same: are you able to achieve the good things you set out to do for each day, and are you able to live peacefully, joyfully and comfortably with yourself each day? If your answer is "no" or "I'm not sure", may I suggest to you that you too, may be faced with the prospect of being powerless over the management of your life.

When I came to my senses, this step was really easy to explain. In a nutshell, I could not manage things in my life that I put my mind and will to managing, and I was powerless over deciding what I wanted to do and how I wanted to feel in each day. This, I can admit.

I believe the Lord showed me – what I mean by *showed* me, is that it became clear and made real sense in my mind's eye – something quite profound in the beginning of my eighth year of sobriety. I am truly thankful to God that I never needed this clarification in the beginning, and neither do you. My new philosophy from God is this:

In my life thus far, I have mistaken God's gift of grace for my self-willed power, and the many talents He has so freely bestowed upon me as my own ability to manage my affairs.

It is only through His gracious gift of discomfort that I became desperate enough to follow this path to freedom, and to actually recognize His gifts of grace and talents that He had given me. I believe that I could go no further in this process until I was able to properly see that I was powerless and that my life was unmanageable by *me*, or indeed by any other person.

The action for Step 1

Working Step 1 is basically two sincere admissions, and you can then move onto Step 2:

1) Can you truly see and admit that you are powerless over yourself?

2) Can you see and admit that your life is unmanageable by *you*?

If by this point you recognize and agree with certain points but cannot bring yourself to admitting powerlessness over yourself and/or the un-manageability of your life, ask God to help you. I do not recommend going any further with the steps until you are able to admit these two things; you will likely be wasting your time if you do so. Stay here and keep praying until the clarity and willingness comes. I have no idea how long that might take, but if you are sincere, it'll come to you. Let me pray for you here:

"Dear heavenly Father, I humbly ask You to open the eyes of this child of Yours who is reading here, so that they may truly see. I ask right now, Lord, for an outpouring of Your precious grace upon them, so that they might be able to make an informed decision on their lives from here on in, and that they can truly admit their powerlessness over themselves and the general unmanageability of the rest of their life. I ask this in the name of Jesus Christ. Amen."

If you are willing to admit your powerlessness over yourself, and that your life is unmanageable by you, let's finish Step 1. Pray a prayer out aloud, something along these lines:

"Dear heavenly Father, thank You that You have brought me to this point in my life. I can now see, and I admit, that I am powerless over myself and that my life is unmanageable for me. In the name of Jesus, I pray. Amen."

Step 2

We came to believe that a power
greater than ourselves could
restore us to sanity.

(Belief)

And he said unto me, My grace is sufficient for thee: for
my strength is made perfect in weakness. Most gladly
therefore will I rather glory in my infirmities, that the
power of Christ may rest upon me. 2 Corinthians 12:9

I feel that if anyone is going to continue and work this step thoroughly, they will need to admit to themselves that they are insane. However, the insanity they told me about when I came into the Program is the insanity of doing the same thing over and over again and expecting a different result each time. The best analogy that springs to mind is that of a fella switching on a light that doesn't come on. He's most perplexed and stares up at the fitting. He then flicks the switch off and switches it on again, at the same time jerking his head up at the ceiling. Still nothing . . . He does it again, slowly, then quickly, thereafter in rapid succession; all to no avail. Ten minutes go by, and he is still switching the switch on and off with as much enthusiasm as when he first started. If someone told me this, I'd probably think that this chap may need a little help. Normally a person would switch it on and off once or twice and then replace the lightbulb or check the fuse board, for example. In other words, they would do something *else* to try to achieve the desired result.

My life followed the same pattern of insanity. You have already read the description I gave of an unmanageable day in my life in the section on Step 1. I never once said to myself that I am going out today to be nasty and miserable, and distant from God; no way! The insanity of my life was this: I would go about my next day in exactly the same manner as the day before, somehow thinking that this time it would be different. I must have convinced myself of this literally thousands of times in my life. Each time the conviction of the thought that things would work out differently was as strong as the last. It was very seldom different and if by chance it was, it always came with the uneasy feeling that something was still not right with the *status quo*. This ties in with exactly what Paul the apostle describes, and I like this version from *The Message*:

> *I can anticipate the response that is coming: "I know that all God's commands are spiritual, but I'm not. Isn't this also your experience?" Yes. I'm full of myself – after all, I've spent a long time in sin's prison. What I don't understand about myself is that I decide one way, but then I act another, doing things I absolutely despise. So if I can't be trusted to figure out what is best for myself and then do it, it becomes obvious that God's command is necessary.* Romans 7:14-16 (MSG)

In the light of this, I was able to admit a certain degree of insanity, and this was enough to get started.

You will see why it is impossible to do Step 2 without having done Step 1. If I was to believe there could be a power greater than myself, I would already have had to admit that whatever power I thought I possessed, would not be as efficient to overcome the problem as this other source of power. For me, the saving grace of this step was in the words "came to believe". This tells me that I do not have to *fully* believe in a power greater than myself straight away.

> *And you were dead in the trespasses and sins in which you once walked, following the course of this world, following the prince of the power of the air, the spirit that is now at work in the sons of disobedience – among whom we all once lived in the passions of our flesh, carrying out the desires of the body and the mind, and were by nature children of wrath, like the rest of mankind. But God, being rich in mercy, because of the great love with which he loved us, even when we were dead in our trespasses, made us alive together with Christ – by grace you have been saved.*
>
> Ephesians 2:1-5 (ESV)

For me, the last sentence is the key; we can proceed even when we are dead in our sins! I'd always thought that I had to attain a semblance of "goodness" or civility before I was worthy enough to approach God, but this just isn't so. We all fall short of the mark, and we cannot change that on our own; we're to come as we are, "warts an' all", so to speak.

I did not need to give this power a name or have any preconceived ideas or notions about what or who it was.

You must remember that at this point in my life I had turned away from Jesus and the church and was now a self-proclaimed agnostic, believing there might be some sort of "force or being" that all religions were praying to and calling a different name. I thought that the "God, Jesus and the Holy Spirit" in the church I knew had done nothing to help me. I'd begged, prayed and pleaded most sincerely, and nothing had happened. You might be able to relate to this and understand why I was feeling more than a little bit sceptical. You see, I had never consciously experienced or been aware of God in my life.

So how did I get over this hurdle? Well, it was with small, but willing steps. I was asked to keep an open mind to the possibility of a power greater than myself, to be as honest as I could, and to be willing to continue the process. I got my strength to do this out of sheer desperation – I'd tried everything else I knew – and enough belief in what these people were saying had worked in their lives, simply because I could relate to key elements within their experiences. I knew they could not be fabricating it, because it is not something a person can invent or repeat with any conviction, unless the person had actually experienced it for themselves. I realized that somehow they had previously been where I was now, and yet they seemed to have a very real relationship with God. They had somehow attained something in their lives that I desperately wanted.

At a meeting many years ago, there was a story shared by a Russian scientist who was an alcoholic, on how he had come to grips with a power greater than himself, and I found this really helped me have a clear and logical understanding and belief in practical, yet unforeseen forces that were beyond my control and strength. He said he would open a bottle of vodka and have two shots out of it. He'd put the bottle on the table and say to himself that that was enough for the night, and yet he said he could not stop himself from finishing the bottle. He thought long and hard about this phenomenon, and eventually said to himself that if this inanimate object wielded a power greater than the strongest willpower he could muster, how much more so could an actual *force or being* do so?

I needed to be *willing* to believe, and the words "Came to believe" suggest to me that we're talking about a journey here. We always start a journey, no matter how great or how small, with the first step. This gave me such hope, to know that I could begin this journey just as I was; "the good, the bad and the ugly", to coin a phrase. I did not have to achieve a certain status before this "power" started doing for me what I was unable to do for myself. I needed as much honesty as I could muster, and I needed to be honest with myself about how much honesty that was, even if it was only minuscule. I also needed to be willing and open-minded to the possibility that God, through Jesus Christ and the Holy Spirit, might reveal Himself to me in a way I had never heard of or seen before – that my beliefs and the preconceived ideas that had been taught to me, or that I thought to be true about our resurrected Lord – might have been seen through my own natural eyes and not through the spiritual eyes God wanted me to see them through, by His Holy Spirit. The way I see God now is totally different from the way I heard ministers, pastors and other Christians speak of Him in their own experiences. I have come to believe and understand that

God has a unique and individual relationship with each of us. I totally agree with what the others say about God if it ties in with scripture; I just perceive it all from a unique angle and I believe this has been given to me by the Holy Spirit. All my preconceived ideas and notions of God were actually blocking me from the power of God. My ego was doing the damage. This is the open-mindedness I'm talking about; I have no expectations on *how* or *when* God's going to work, I'm just willing to hand over and give it a go.

The other beautiful thing about this Program, and indeed this step, is that my best doesn't have to be very good at all; it could be horrid, in fact. Everything I have said up until this point might make no sense to you at all. You could be saying to yourself, "This chap is on another planet!" That does not mean you can't move into relationship with God from right now until the day you die. It does not mean that if you move out of relationship with Him that all is lost. You have another ten steps to go. The promise is that this Program does work; with some of us it works quickly and with others slowly, but it does work. My prayer is that God's grace will have allowed you by now to grab onto something that you can *relate* to, and that this will fuel your hope. All you need is the willingness to continue to the end. Again, remember that this is a journey, and the journey is lifelong, and is one of the most awesome journeys you could ever take – it's exciting! Where I am now, I am glad there is so much more. To me, it's like a good novel or an enjoyable holiday. You are so into it that the thought of it ending is unbearable. I pray it will be like this for you too. The journey, once started, continues for our whole lives, but when we die, it's like the sequel – to be continued in heaven for eternity.

The action for Step 2

Like in Step 1, there are two things you need to agree on in your mind:

1) Are you able to sincerely admit your insanity (doing the same things over and over again expecting a different result)?

2) Can you keep an open mind to the possibility of a power greater than yourself that can restore you to your sanity?

If you understand and can accept this, we can proceed.

Let us pray together:

"Dear heavenly Father, give me the strength to be willing and open-minded towards You, without placing any expectations on Your workings. I know that I do not have the power within me to restore sanity into my life. I realize the insanity of my situation and want to trust You to restore me to my sanity, so that I will ultimately be of maximum service to You and can have a personal relationship with You, one which is unique to me. I ask this in the name of Jesus Christ. Amen."

Step 3

We made a decision to turn our will
and our lives over to the care of God,
through Jesus Christ.

(Decision)

*And he said to them all, If any man will come after me,
let him deny himself, and take up his cross daily, and
follow me.*   Luke 9:23

I faced a dilemma at this point in the process: how could
I make a decision to hand my will and my life over to
something I didn't fully trust yet?

The first help came from the fact that I had exhausted all
other avenues in my attempt to run my life. I was desperate
to try anything, and I had enough faith in what I read and
saw in the Program to prompt me to give it a sincere try.

The second help came from one of my first sponsors
(mentors) in the Program. He said that I should not focus
too much on understanding and believing in this power,
that the decision to hand my will and life over to Him could
be enforced if I continued with the rest of the steps to the

best of my ability. What a relief! I was able to make the decision to turn my will and my life over to the care of God by simply making the decision to see these steps through to the end.

It worked like this for me; as soon as I was able to grasp Step 2 and the possibility of something out there more powerful than me, Step 3 was easy and just had to be formalized.

My understanding of God and how it all works is now very different to what it was when I did this step. Here is a summary of what I now believe:

- He is the *only* God, the all-powerful creator of the universe.

- He is made up of God the Father, God the Son and God the Holy Spirit, yet they are one. I don't fully understand this but believe enough to accept this as so.

- Because of the deceit of Satan (Lucifer – the devil), the entire human race has sinned and is doomed to an eternity of separation from our creator – God. We are unlikely to fully understand the concept of "hell", but separation is something we can more easily grasp.

- Because of the immense love God has for us (again, something we cannot grasp in its fullness), He provided a way out for us. He made the ultimate sacrifice for us by giving of Himself (His Son), to become a mortal man and live a blameless life amongst us. His Son, Jesus Christ, who had to be blameless, took our sins upon Himself and was put to death. He paid the price for the penalty of our sin. The pain God the Father must have felt to have to turn Himself away from His Son at this point is something else that is hard to fully comprehend.

- Because of Jesus' innocence and power, He overcame the grave and was resurrected to life, and is now seated at the right hand of God the Father. Not only that, but He is speaking and pleading with the Father on our behalf.

- We have to play our part, and Jesus wants to see each one of us make the right choice. Every one of us has to do the following in order to receive the benefit of this enormous sacrifice: we need to confess with our mouths and believe in our hearts that Jesus Christ died on the cross for our sins, that He rose again on the third day, and that He is now seated at the right hand of God the Father and is interceding on our behalf. We also have to repent (meaning turning away from, and towards God) of our sins. If we do this, we will spend eternity in heaven with God. We have no way of fully comprehending what heaven will be like, but it will be joyous, free from fear, worry, heartache, pain, strife and misery. There is nothing more (or less) that I need to do to receive this.

- The reason God created us was so that He could have a *real* relationship with us. He loves us and has given us the choice to love Him back; we are an expression of God's love.

I needed the journey of alcoholism to get me desperate enough to seek God *with all my heart.*[27] His grace, through the medium of alcoholism, opened my eyes so that I could see the truth. Then the choice was easy for me, but I still had to make the actual decision.

However, this is a far cry from what I understood God to be back then. Just making the decision, based on the little I knew, to hand over my will and life to Him was enough to set me off in the direction of where I am today: truly joyous and free, and still growing. This is the beginning, and God can move into relationship with you in an instant; He certainly did with me. In the past I have noticed that he has not always worked that way in other people I've known and taken through the Program. Some of them struggled a time, but all of those who eventually found themselves in deep relationship with God, worked through the steps to the end. I believe that had I stopped working through this Program at the point when I started to feel peace, joy and contentment in my life, I would not have established the foundation needed to sustain a permanent intimate relationship with God. Our character defects are patient; none more so than pride, ego and self. Paul says to the church in Corinth:

And lest I should be exalted above measure through the abundance of the revelations, there was given to me a thorn in the flesh, the messenger of Satan to buffet me, lest I should be exalted above measure.

2 Corinthians 12:7

27. Please bear in mind that not everyone will be that self-absorbed or stubborn that they would need something of this magnitude to get them to earnestly seek.

I believe that Paul was talking of pride here, something I know all about. For me, my "thorn in the flesh" is that I am still an alcoholic, and if I pick up a drink, I will be back to square one. This fact means that I have to remain in a relationship with the Lord every day, which is what God wants from me; from each of us, I believe.

Getting to know someone takes time – time you will have to spend with that person. Firstly, though, you need to make a decision to actually get to know that person. Once you have made that decision, you still will not know them unless you call them up to make arrangements and then go and meet them and spend time with them. In the beginning you will only know them a little, but the more time you spend with them, the better you will get to know them. You would not expect to know everything about this person from one or two meetings, but you will be moving in the right direction. I believe that "Satan"[28] (the devil) wanted to take me out with this "thorn" of alcoholism. However, he did not consider what the scriptures say:

And we know that all things work together for good to them that love God, to them that are the called according to His purpose. Romans 8:28

I feel that the Lord has used the very "thorn" that drove me away from Him to actually bring me into and keep me in a relationship with Him that is much stronger and closer than it ever was. But I had to surrender my will over to Him; I had to make that decision myself. Living my own way

---

28. You do not need to believe in a conventional devil for these steps, but just have an open-mindedness to the possibility of some force that seems to pull you in the wrong direction at times.

with my own plans was just not working (remember the diesel Audi story[29]).

We make the decision that God's will shall be done and admit that our way never worked.

The action for Step 3

When you have really made the decision in your mind to turn your will and your life over to the care of God, say this prayer out aloud, with all the sincerity you have at your disposal:

> "God, I offer myself to You – to build me and to do with me as You will. Relieve me of the bondage of self, that I may better do Your will. Take away my difficulties, that victory over them might bear witness to those I would help of Your power, Your love and Your way of life. May I do Your will always. In the name of Jesus Christ. Amen."

This is Step 3 completed. It's quite simple once you make up your mind, but I believe it is one of the most powerful decisions to make.

You may proceed to Step 4, but please remember one important point: you should have no preconceived ideas as to how and when God will work – just work through the steps as honestly and sincerely as possible.

---

29. See page 54.

Step 4

We made a searching and fearless moral inventory of ourselves.

(Practicality)

Let us search and try our ways, and turn again to the LORD.   Lamentations 3:40

I thank the Lord for the honesty He has given me in being able to share all the things of my life with you so openly; it's been liberating for me, and I trust that you will be able to relate to some of the situations and feelings on a personal level. It was not like this for me in the beginning. If you are scared to death about bringing all your "dirty laundry" out on paper, I want you to know that I felt the same. In fact, there are things from my past of which I am still not strong enough to share with you in this book. The wonderful thing is that at this stage of Step 4 I never had to in order to find freedom and peace. I was asked to make a searching and fearless moral inventory of *myself*, not of somebody else, and not have my inventory done by someone else either. I can tell you that the thought of doing this step sent shivers down my spine, but I was desperate, and at least I knew no one else had to see my inventory – yet.

When it was spelled out for me in this step that I was going to have to "clean house" in order to move into a deeper relationship with the Lord, I remembered that this had sub-consciously been one of the main reasons that had held me back from seeking God in the first place. I hated myself for what I believed I'd become and for what I felt I stood for. This step was asking me to bring it all up and put it on paper, and I really did not want to do it. Once again, however, it was God's grace in the form of desperation that pushed me forwards.

Perhaps through reading my journey into alcoholism, you recognize that you are on the same path. You may not have the alcohol addiction, but you might be able to relate to some of the feelings and fears I have shared. It may be that all you are feeling is a sense of uneasiness or detachment from others, God, or both. I pray that this will create a sense of hope and anticipation in you so that you are able to work this step before you slip further into despair.

You will see throughout this book that I often refer to either self, ego or pride as being our main problem and the cause of all our other defects of character. C.S. Lewis refers to pride as the "Great Sin".[30] I could not word it better and I see this so clearly now. What I can add from my own experience is that a person suffering with pride cannot see it in themselves, no matter how much it is pointed out to them; they simply cannot. This Program was a process for me that brought me to a place where I could recognize my pride. It is easy to see pride in others, but we are not to take another person's inventory – this is very important to remember.

---

30. *Mere Christianity* by C.S. Lewis © copyright 1942, 1942, 1944, 1952 C.S. Lewis Pte Ltd.

"What has all this to do with our searching and fearless moral inventory?" you may ask. Well, it shows us the root-cause of all our other wrongs. In a nutshell, we will come to see that the nature of our faults of character can be summed up into five. We are:

- selfish;

- self-centred;

- dishonest;

- afraid;

- inconsiderate.

All these defects stem from pride, ego and self. We cannot see all this just yet, but this Program is, as the late Charles Chamberlin said, "a process of uncover, discover and discard".[31] In this step we are *uncovering*. We want to see how, when, where and with whom we have been wrong, so that we can get on course to rectifying these character defects and the trouble they've caused. It would be pointless to try to fix something if we never knew what was wrong with it. Why do we need to bother with these things, which might be hidden deep in us and painful to extract? It's because they cut us off from the only effective power source, which is God, who is the very One we are trying to form a relationship with in the first place.

There are four areas we are going to break down and look at in the working part of this step, and they are our *resentments, fears, harms* and *good qualities*. We need to get them down on paper to look at them, and we should

31. Charles Chamberlin, speaking at a men's retreat in Pala Mesa in 1975.

do so as thoroughly as possible. At the time I thought this idea of getting it all down on paper unnecessary, but I did it anyway. I later found out I was wrong, and now believe it to be a very important part of the process. Don't worry, everything will be explained and tabled for you; there will even be lists of prompts to help get your memory going.

There are three main objectives we are trying to achieve here. Firstly, we are trying to establish what these four things affect in us. Secondly, it is to establish what our part is; the exact nature behind where we were wrong. Our good qualities may be slightly challenging, as it is often more difficult to uncover our true motive for doing good things. We want good qualities with good motives at the end of the day. If our motives are good but our qualities appear bad, we can rest assured this will be righted, as God is looking at our hearts. I don't want you to feel despondent though; all of us have genuine good qualities given to us by God. If you can't find them, it is probably because they've been clouded over by the character defects, or they have become warped and exploited over time. When we are thoroughly done with this Program, the good qualities will start to come back, and new ones will form. Lastly, we decide to make the best possible amends and restitution with others (where possible), but most importantly with God, as we ask Him to help and strengthen us.

Some encouragement and support

Take your time with this step; there is no rush. I found that thoroughness in this step has been invaluable to me in setting a solid foundation. Do a bit each day or when you get a chance, and you'll be spending quality time with God without even realizing it. As you start on Step 4, you may have felt overwhelmed at the thought of doing the inventory lists; ask for God's strength in a simple prayer:

"Lord, I am too weak and scared to go any further. Please give me the strength to continue with this step; thank You. I ask this in the name of Jesus. Amen."

Once you've said this prayer, don't sit back. Read through the step and start by doing what you can; start with the easy ones. If you are asked to list your resentments, list the ones that come easily to you. You may resent your old school for making you wear funny hats to sports days. Write it down! Then think of the next easy one. You may be resentful towards a work colleague who spread rumours about you so that he could win a promotion position over you. Write it down! Continue like this. Remember that you need to start *doing* something, and if you're doing what you can, the rest will follow.

Even so faith, if it hath not works, is dead, being alone.

James 2:17

I suggest you look up that scripture and read the whole chapter; it really gives clarity and understanding.

This is the first step where action is needed. We are now going to start sorting out the mental, emotional, physical and spiritual issues of our past, up to and including the present day. Don't be overwhelmed when you look at it, we take things one day at a time in this Program. Do you know how to eat a whole elephant? One bite at a time! The point is this, it does not matter how long it takes, it's that you do it that counts.

You do not necessarily need to complete the Program before you start to sense that something is happening. God is all-powerful, and if your heart is right, you may start to sense elements of His presence straight away. It often happens in the Program that someone starts to feel a sense of ease and comfort without having worked through all the steps, and when that happens, very often they do not want to continue to do all the steps in the Program because they think it will hurt too much, and actually, they feel okay now. So, feeling liberated, that person may decide that some of the steps are enough for them, and they are happy where they are at now. If this happens to you I suggest you don't be fooled by the "pink cloud" experience. If you want to maintain what you now have, you're going to have to clean house. Picture a ship being tossed around at sea as your life. You find the Program and maybe start the first couple of steps. This is like your ship anchoring in the harbour. Compared to being tossed around in turmoil out at sea, being docked in the harbour is calm and blissful. In my job I've always been told that "good is the enemy of best". I can say the same for this scenario. Being in the Program and experiencing a few months with a semblance of peace, joy and contentment may feel like heaven. You think to yourself that it couldn't get better than this. If the truth be told, though, you're actually still scared of working through all the steps. I have met so many in the Program that never get past Step 3; we call it the "three-step waltz" because they would rather go back and do the first three steps again: one-two-three, one-two-three, one-two-three, round and round they go. But they cannot see the beauty and freedom of actually stepping ashore; the freedom and peace that comes with completing the steps. It would be okay to remain like this in the peaceful harbour I guess, if it weren't for the fact that ships leave harbours and sail out to rough seas again. If you're still on that boat, you're going off again. If you're wanting to achieve a truly deep and meaningful relationship with God this process needs to run its full course, and you will need to step ashore. Moreover, God has something so much bigger in store for you – He has for us all if we let Him.

This need to work through the steps was daunting for me as well, especially Step 4. I didn't know where to start. Over the years, I have developed some systems (guidance from the Holy Spirit, I believe) that have worked for me, and have found worksheets that I've modified, breaking this step into very doable "bite-sizes". You may not understand all aspects of the steps because you are probably working them on your own, and although I'll try to answer your email queries, it might still be confusing for you. That is why I have tried to go into great detail, cramming as many suggestions into the book as possible.

Do not lose heart. I suggest you follow the action steps like you would a cake recipe; that's how I did it because I was totally desperate initially, which made me worried that if I did not get it just right, I may miss out on what others had clearly received. I am so glad I did it that way, because I feel I got the best foundation possible. You will need to be as thorough as you can possibly be. In a cake recipe, for instance, it may say "a cup of white flour". You look in the pantry and you see you only have three quarters of a cup and decide that will do. It says, "5 tablespoons of white sugar" and you only have brown, so you use it. It says "3 eggs" but you like eggs and decide to add four. It says, "bake at 180°C for 30 minutes", but you are now hungry and don't want to wait, so you push it to 200°C for 15 minutes. When your cake comes out, I guarantee it will be a flop. It's the same with the Program. Follow each suggestion as it is laid out. I have aimed to put as much into the steps as possible. If the recipe said three eggs, I have tried to give you the actual size of the eggs as well, so to speak. You will encounter things about which you are just not sure; pray and ask God for direction and then do what you think is most right. The Lord sees your heart, and He can help you even without your effort. I believe He really wants to see that you are honest and sincere. If you are, it will come.

I am convinced that not having a deep and personal relationship with God will forever leave us as humans feeling restless, irritable and discontent. You could leave out this step until it gets really bad, but who knows if you'll get another chance? However, if you are feeling as I was, you will probably not be enjoying your life anyway. Whatever your conviction may be, I pray that you will be able to make this inventory as best you can.

Glossary and explanation of key words

Below is a small glossary of words used and their basic meanings according to the understanding I gained when I worked through the Program. In some cases, I have emphasized the meanings of the words in the context of our working of this step, so the explanations given here may differ a little from some dictionary definitions. As such, I suggest you read through them, even if you know the meanings. On occasion I find that something worded differently can add new insight.

If need be, use this section as a point of reference while doing this step. I would suggest taking a moment to look back to the meaning of a word as it is written here, rather than not being sure and continuing with the step. I have found in my own experience that it has given me a sound grasp of the meaning needed in the context of completing this step, and also for daily inventories done in the spur of the moment (as will be covered in Step 10).

Inventories

Resentment(s) Feelings of bitter hurt or indignation (anger – excited by assumptions made), which come from rightly or wrongfully held feelings of being injured or offended (wrong judgement).

Fear(s) Feelings of anxiety, agitation, uneasiness, apprehension, dread, worry, etc. (wrong belief).

Harm(s) Wrong acts which result in pain, hurt feelings, worry, financial loss, etc.; these towards others and self (wrong action).

Good qualities Qualities within us that appear naturally, that generally bless, help, uplift or benefit others to another person's ultimate advantage.

Motive   My true purpose when benefitting someone else (including God); whether with little or no thought to any gain for myself in any way (good motive) or doing something with the intention of gaining something for myself (this is often a sub-conscious attitude), which could include personal satisfaction (wrong motive).

Our Defects of Character (wrongs)

Selfish   When I am deficient in my consideration of others (can be conscious or unconscious), giving primary attention to my own agenda, while paying little or no attention to anyone else's agenda or well-being, or putting mine before theirs.

Self-seeking   Occupied mainly with my own affairs, seeking mainly or solely to further my own interests. The difference here between selfish and self-seeking, is that it may or may not involve other people, and in many instances can be something that others actually benefit from. However, in being self-seeking, the other person may actually have been given consideration, but the true primary beneficiary would be oneself.

Dishonest   The act of not telling the truth, lying, cheating, stealing, deceiving, telling half-truths, or sometimes not speaking up when I know that the truth might shed light on a subject, thereby changing the outlook or outcome.

Frightened   Being in a temporary or continual state of fear, which includes all or some of the feelings of anxiety, agitation, uneasiness, apprehension, dread, worry, etc.

Inconsiderate Not taking the time to consider any understandable scenarios as to why another person may have behaved the way they had in any specific situation that ultimately hurt or upset us.[32]

We will now deal with each of our inventories one at a time: resentments, fears, harms and good qualities. You might feel that there is a lot of reading and instructions here, but do not be discouraged, as most of it is to help you understand what to do in the best way possible. Your actual work is on the worksheet and is quite short, while the other is prompts, suggestions and instructions to help you to complete the worksheets and to be able to get the best possible overview of where you have been before.

I pray that the Holy Spirit open your eyes to reveal His truth to you about yourself, just as He did for me.

---

32. Please note that just because we create a scenario that helps us understand why someone acted the way they did, it would not necessarily excuse the person's behaviour or reaction.

I recommend that you read everything carefully and do what it says to the best of your ability. You will see that in each inventory, I have given one or two of my own personal inventory examples in the worksheets, with explanations of how and why I came to tick whichever box. I have done this so that you might get a feel of how I produced my inventory. However, if you do yours slightly differently or have a different way of reasoning, that is completely fine. We are all different people, and it is amazing that God works with us and through us to suit our own unique design. Who better, seeing as He made us with our individual personalities? Throughout this Program, the key is to be as honest, open and as willing as we can possibly be.

Let us now take a look at each of the four areas mentioned, individually.

Resentments

Resentments are feelings of bitter hurt or indignation which come from rightly or wrongly held feelings of being injured or offended. I have often heard it said that "resentment is like drinking poison and expecting the other person to die". There was a chap with quite a sense of humour at one of the meetings, who used to say, "Resentment is like pouring petrol all over yourself, lighting it, and then hoping the other fella will choke to death in the fumes!" The person holding the resentment is always worse off than the person/institution/principle against which the resentment is held. In the book *Alcoholics Anonymous,* Bill Wilson (co-founder) said that resentment is the number-one destroyer of alcoholics. I believe that resentment plays a major part in blocking us off from true fellowship with the Lord. The reason I believe this to be so is that in most cases, the person holding onto the resentment is feeling that they are the aggrieved party, that they are the one who has been hurt, rightfully or not. This means that they are unable or unwilling to want to bring restitution to the relationship with the other. Sometimes, after finding out more facts, we can discover that in fact we were not wronged after all.

For example, consider the case of two office ladies, Anne and Julia, having a conversation. Anne tells Julia something in confidence. Two days later, Anne hears another lady from the office, Mary, talking about the same topic. Anne feels very resentful towards Julia for what she believes to be gossip and breaking of trust. After a few days, however, Mary mentions to Anne that the office partition walls are very thin and that she overheard her chatting with Julia. So, was Anne's resentment justified? What if, despite Mary overhearing the conversation, Julia did in fact also go and share the news with her? In this case, some would consider Anne's resentment to be justified, although it depends somewhat on your point of view. What is clear, however, is that justified or not, Anne was carrying resentment and she was the one suffering because of it.

Any resentment is destructive to you, and you need to get rid of it. For me, justified resentment was the hardest to deal with. I loved brooding and festering over a nice big, fat, juicy – "justified resentment". If I had had a bad day, I'd get home and haul that old resentment out and play it over and over in my mind until I felt better about myself, and ready to really give that "low-life" a piece of my mind. Just putting it on paper here and reading it now highlights to me how "insane" I was and sometimes still am, I must add.

When we look at our resentments, we will put each one into a table, which you'll see in the working section of the book – all nice and easy. We will look at three things:

- Who caused the resentment?

- What about the situation caused the resentment?

- What was my part in the establishment of this resentment?

Firstly, you write down the person/institution/principle that were the cause, then you write what is really bugging you about the scenario, and finally you check your part against the five major character defects: have I been selfish, self-seeking, dishonest, frightened or inconsiderate? You may have one, all or a combination of a few of these character defects for each of your listed resentments. If you have resentment, you *will* certainly have at least one of these character defects. To a greater or lesser degree, the resentment you carry will have impacted your character. If the thought of this "work" is making you feel a little apprehensive, there are worksheets, prompts and real-life step-for-step examples, so you should have full clarity.

When I was doing my Step 4 for the second time, I remember explaining to my sponsor that I had resentment where I felt I was fully justified in having it. I then proceeded to explain that in South Africa there are these minibus taxis. (If you are a South African, you will already be saying, "I know where this is going . . .") They are an absolute menace on the roads. I would like to check the traffic bylaws of SA one day, because I'm sure there must be two sets of road rules: one for the minibus taxis and one for everyone else. The solid yellow lines forming hard shoulders on the sides of the roads are for emergency vehicles only. The minibus taxis act as if it is an extra taxi lane in peak-hour traffic. They are the cause of innumerable accidents; they swerve in front of cars, cut people off, stop anywhere they like when someone on the walkway signals for them to stop, and so on. When they do this in front of me and I have to brake hard and swerve with screeching tyres trying to avoid smashing into them, a "little" resentment forms. My blood boils over and I use some inappropriate colourful language, accompanied by a few of the local traffic "hand signs" which are used for such cases! (I have improved over time and now include them in my prayers – I also have to ask the Lord's forgiveness almost daily, and I thank Him for His gracious mercy.) Someone once complimented a lady for her generous heart by saying, "Gertrude's heart is like a minibus taxi; there's always room for one more." (Just something I thought very funny at the time!) Minibus taxis are similar and tend to stop wherever to cram another passenger in.

My sponsor then put a scenario to me. He asked if I'd considered whether the taxi driver had a wife and large family to support; and what if that taxi driver's boss had said to him that if he didn't do ten full trips a day he'd get fired. He asked me that if I knew that to be true, whether I would still feel resentful towards him? I thought for a moment and had to say that I would not. Sure, I'd be cross initially, but then I'd probably let it go. You see, I had been inconsiderate of his situation and perhaps a little fearful of the possible danger. (That is not to say that he *does* have a wife and large family to support, with his job on the line – but it is possible.)

To illustrate this further, I want you to picture yourself on an overnight bus (not a minibus!) travelling from one city to another. A man gets on with his two kids of about six and eight. He sits next to another passenger against the window, while the two kids sit one row back on the opposite side of the aisle. You are a further two rows behind the children. The bus pulls off and everybody settles down to sleep. The bus has hardly left the city, when the kids start with their restlessness; bickering, hitting each other and shrieking. People are starting to stare in the direction of the father who is sitting with his head against the glass, staring blankly at nothing. He seems completely unfazed by his children's bad behaviour, even when they start running up and down the aisle shouting and screaming. You sit there flabbergasted by the fact that the father is not trying to control his unruly kids.

You've been trying to sleep but cannot, and you've almost had enough, when a woman sitting behind him gets up and angrily taps the father on his shoulder. "Can't you keep your kids quiet? There are people trying to sleep on this bus," she blurts out.

"Too right!" you think to yourself.

The man stands up and, loudly enough for everyone to hear, he says, "I am so sorry and do apologize to everyone for my absentmindedness. We've just come from the hospital where their mother has passed away; my thoughts have been elsewhere, but I will sort them out right now. I apologize for any inconveniences my children may have caused."

Can you imagine the first thought you'd have? My first thought would be, "Thank goodness I never said anything!" Also, I think that if the kids became unruly again, I don't think it would bother me as much, how about you? I might even try to help by telling them a story or giving them a cookie or something.

What changed? Nothing really, except we'd received information about the situation that we had not considered when we first made a judgement call, and this was enough to remove any traces of resentment we felt towards the children and their father. The woman who had "straightened him out" would surely now be making humble apologies and telling him that it is fine and everything was okay now.

In the list of the five defects of character, you had only been inconsiderate, but as soon as more information was given about the situation, you became considerate and the resentment disappeared; amazing, wouldn't you say?

If we're considering a resentment and can't identify where we may have been selfish, self-centred, dishonest or afraid, then I would say we were probably inconsiderate. When going through our resentments, we should try to create possible scenarios in our minds in which the behaviour we felt resentful about would be understandable. Note I said *understandable,* not acceptable. As long as you are trying to understand, you are being considerate, and the resentment will probably leave you.

The action for Step 4's resentments

Resentments Inventory

Download the free Resentments Inventory worksheet,[33] or draw up a blank template on a piece of paper from my example on page 149. Make as many copies as you need; I had 67 resentments when I did this inventory the second time around.

Follow and read quickly through my personal example of the Resentments Inventory example and worksheet on pages 147 to 149. As you go through each stage and complete each column, you can refer back to this example; I have tried to put detailed reasoning for each point. Remember that you will not need to write down your reasoning as I have done; you only have to fill in the worksheets. The only reason I put them down is because I wanted to give you an idea as to the way you might need to think about each point. It's only a guide though; you might have a very different outlook and understanding to mine and that is fine. The important thing to remember is to be as sincere and as thorough as you can; God will take care of the rest. On page 150 you will see a prompt sheet that you can refer back to, and this is to help stimulate memories of possible resentments that may have been forgotten or overlooked over time. Don't get too concerned about doing it "perfectly"; allow God to guide you. For me, He guided me with a niggling thought, an idea or an understanding, which I've tried to explain in the example. When I asked my sponsor if I should or shouldn't put something down

---

33. https://www.malcolmdown.co.uk/worksheets

or answer "yes" to a point, he would ask, "How free do you want to be?" My suggestion to you will be the same; if you're not sure of something, put it down or mark "yes"; you will understand why in your own way as you progress.

How I filled in my first resentment

Column

1. My mother

2. My mum used to say that she did not want me at times because she could not handle me, and it made me feel like I was a mistake and that I was not really wanted.

3. Was I . . .

    - *Selfish?* – no, because being wanted by your mum is a natural desire.

    - *Self-seeking?* – yes, I wanted to be wanted for myself, not thinking what my mother wanted (in the column, I put <u>Self-seeking</u>).

    - *Dishonest?* – yes, I was always being false, trying to show myself as what I thought people wanted me to be, such as saying I liked romantic movies because some girl I was trying to impress did (in the column, I put <u>Dishonest</u>).

    - *Frightened?* – yes, because I had all sorts of fears of rejection and abandonment (in the column, I put <u>Frightened</u>).

- *Inconsiderate?* – yes, because I never considered my mother was 20 years old, stuck in a town more than 1,000 km from her family and help, with a child that was riddled with colic and screamed most of the time (in the column, I put <u>Inconsiderate</u>).

4.   I express my will to make amends to God, which will be through prayer and meditation, by writing <u>Prayer</u> and also <u>Meditation</u>; and to my mother by some way still to be determined at a later stage in Step 8, I write <u>Amends</u>.

Personal Example of My Resentments Inventory Worksheet

	1. The resentment	2. The reason or cause	3. My part	4. Future action
	I am resentful towards (or at) . . .	I am resentful because . . ., and it made me feel. . . .	Was I selfish, self-seeking, dishonest, frightened or inconsiderate in any way?	I will . . . pray and meditate / think and make amends
1.	My mum	My mum used to say that she did not want me at times because she could not handle me, and it made me feel like I was a mistake and that I was not really wanted.	I was: self-seeking, dishonest, frightened and inconsiderate	Pray, meditate and make amends
2.	Girl from England	Broke up with me and left for England the next day, and this made me feel used, and that she never cared about me.	I was: selfish, self-seeking, frightened and inconsiderate	Pray, meditate and make amends
3.	Education system	They don't have proper grants for tertiary education, and this made me feel that they only look after the privileged and, therefore, I was not seen as privileged enough.	I was: self-seeking, frightened and inconsiderate	Pray and meditate
4.	God/deity	He's the boss, I must follow the rules but had no choice in being born or not. I felt incredibly frustrated that I was effectively being forced to choose God or go to hell.	I was: selfish, self-seeking, frightened and inconsiderate	Pray, meditate and make amends
5.	and you continue . . .			

Resentments Inventory Worksheet Prompts

People

Father
(incl. step/in-laws)
Mother
(incl. step/in-laws)
Sisters
(incl. step/in-laws)
Brothers
(incl. step/in-laws)
Aunts
Uncles
Cousins
Clergy (priests,
pastors, etc.)
Police
Lawyers/judges
Doctors
Employers
Employees (if you are
a boss)
Friends (school, best,
life-long)
Teachers
Co-workers
Acquaintances (sexual
and non-sexual)
Girl/boyfriends or
spouses
Parole/probation
officers
Program and rehab
friends
Creditors

Institutions

Marriage
Bible
Church
Religion
Races (general or
specific)
Law
Authority
Government
Education system
Correctional
system
Mental health
system
Philosophy
Nationality
Military
Government
departments
Rehabilitation
centres
Hospitals

Principles

God/deity
(the creator)
Retribution
(vengeance)
The Ten
Commandments
Jesus Christ
Satan
Death
Life after death
Heaven
Hell
Sin
Adultery
A golden rule
("You must . . .")
Original sin
(Adam and Eve)
Seven deadly sins
Eternity
"Do unto
others . . ."
"Turn the other
cheek"

You might have others that spring to mind because these have triggered a memory. Put them on your Resentments Inventory worksheet.

Practical steps for resentments

1) Get your Resentments worksheet out next to you with a pencil. I did my worksheets with a pencil because it was easy to make changes; this helps when you review what you've written, and avoids a lot of scratching and crossing out, which can create confusion.

2) Write down *all* your resentments that you can think of under the first column ("I am resentful towards . . ."), without doing anything to the other columns. Your resentments must include any you have had before, even if you feel you don't have them anymore. If you cannot remember a name, fill in something that will remind you of that specific resentment, e.g. "The women in the lime-green jumper that I met at the village tavern one New Year's party." I suggest that you write down all those that come to mind now.

3) After you have written all the resentments you can think of, read through the Resentments Inventory Worksheet Prompts found on page 150, filling in any resentments that now spring to mind from the prompts which you may not already have written down from memory. Just follow on from the ones you already have in column 1 (you will see the prompt sheet includes people, institutions and principles).

4) Write down in the second column the reason or cause next to each resentment taken from column 1 ("I am resentful because . . ."), as well as how it

made you feel, without doing anything in the other columns. You really just need a brief summary of what actually got "under your skin" so that you'll be able to recall the situation in full in Step 5. Work from top to bottom of column 2 next to each resentment you wrote down in column 1.

Now you will work to the end of every resentment line one at a time, across each of the columns 3 and 4 to the end before going onto the next resentment. I have gone through one of my resentments word-for-word, taking time to put down my thoughts and feelings (see page 147), but you do not need to do this part. It merely suggests the thought process taken; you need only fill the worksheets.

5) Go on to column 3 and ask yourself what part you had to play in the establishment of that specific resentment. For each resentment, write down what you feel your character defect(s) are and underline each one. Going forward, each place where it is suggested you underline, it is so it stands out for you when you review, and this will hopefully highlight the significance of these words for future observation, thought and prayer. Ask yourself whether you were selfish, self-seeking, dishonest, frightened or inconsiderate; a combination of a few of them, or all of them. I do not believe you will leave them all out, because I don't believe a person can have resentments without having at least one of the five defects of character. If you cannot mark any, there is undoubtedly something you have not considered (it might even be hypothetical consideration you never thought of) about the other person, institution or

principle. Ask God for His guidance in revealing what it might be and then put down <u>Inconsiderate</u> underlined, opposite that specific resentment in column 3, and move on to column 4 with that specific resentment.

6) By filling in column 4 we are only making our work easier for Steps 8 and 9. You are not going to do any work here; you are merely displaying a willingness to "clean your side of the street". I do not believe we should mark down an amends to the person, institution or principle, if nothing disrespectful was done towards them (i.e. you never harmed them in any way). If you have though, you will put down <u>Amends</u> underlined. I believe we will always have hurt God, so we show our willingness to ask God for forgiveness by putting down <u>Prayer</u> and <u>Meditation</u>, and we underline the words.

You have now completed your Resentments Inventory. Well done! I know it is a lot, but I found it vital, and I urge you to keep going, it gets easier from here on in.

Alan's Story

I became a Christian about fifteen years ago, and since then I have always had a sincere trust that because I accepted and believed what Jesus did for me on the cross, I have salvation and that I will go to heaven one day to spend eternity with God. Making this commitment was a profound moment in my life, and I have built up a level of trust and relationship with God over the years. However, there seemed to be an underlying niggle and thought that there was something missing, and that I really sensed there was a lack of true intimacy with God. It wasn't an awful feeling, but just a sense that there was so much more to God and Christianity that I was missing out on.

In our church I heard of a course, "Entering into a deeper relationship with God", which was starting up and I was intrigued to find out if this could help me overcome the niggle I had been feeling, and so I joined the group. When I started the course, which was based around this step-program, I heard a bit being mentioned about dependency disorders, and I was a little unsure how a twelve-step system used to address dependency disorders could help me. I didn't have any dependency disorders (or so I thought at the time), but the title of the course was compelling and something that I wanted to strive for, so I continued with it.

We got to a section that dealt with our defects of character. There was one on resentments, and I mentioned to Rory after one of the meetings that I was not someone who really held resentments. He suggested I pray and ask God to reveal any that I may not be aware of and that if there weren't any, I could just continue going through the other defects of character. I did this and, much to my surprise, it quickly became clear that I had built up many resentments that had damaged my relationships with people and had also put up barriers that prevented God having free rule in my life.

The course gave me a set of tools that enabled me to identify and to address the resentments I had built up. More importantly, it showed me how to make amends to the people I had hurt, and to God, who I was sinning against by the attitudes I had developed. It was really helpful to do this as part of a group. I found that as the course went on and trust between group members developed, we were able to share our stories, sometimes for the first time in our lives, and this was of great encouragement to us all. Because of this we were able to support each other when support was needed.

Rory describes our relationship with God as being like a conduit that connects us to Him. His love, which comes through the power of the Holy Spirit, flows down that conduit to us, and then that love flows from us to others around us. Through the unconscious resentments I had allowed to build up over the years I had caused this conduit to become blocked, thereby limiting my relationship with God and with others. As the blockages were cleared up through the process of the Program, I felt the Holy Spirit moving more in my life than I had felt for years, and there is no doubt that my relationship with God has moved into a new level of intimacy. Through this closer relationship I now experience with God, I get a real sense that as long as I keep the conduit of my life clear and continue to trust and obey Him, He will remain in control of my life, and He will grow and deepen our relationship as He sees fit; there is no other effort required on my part. Another thing that I have come to understand and realize is that anything I turn to and rely or depend on before I do God, is a dependency disorder. I need to turn and depend on Him for everything.

I know I am far from perfect and there is still a lot of work to do. I still find myself resenting people because of their words or actions. Thankfully, the course provides me with a simple condensed version of the process in Step 10, which only takes a few minutes to do each time. Using this enables me to address the resentments before they become sin, and this keeps me in relationship with God. The process has helped me to understand with greater clarity how sin damages our relationship with God, and how using the 12-step process taught on the course gives a workable solution that helps me stay on track. I will always be grateful for the insight God has given in this program, and for its impact on my life and on the lives of all who have done the work contained in it.

Fears

Fears are feelings of anxiety, agitation, uneasiness, apprehension, etc. Yes, fear is also sin and will cut you off from God just like the others. Fear is one that I still struggle with immensely. To be more specific, I battle with the fear of rejection. I have come to understand that fear is there in my life because, quite simply, I do not trust God, which means that I have unwittingly placed my trust or dependency in something else, which will ultimately prove fallible.

One of my sponsors, "American Mike", as he is affectionately known, told me of his sponsor who lived in one of the southern states in America. Mike would call him up to say he was worried about something or other. His sponsor's response would be, "Michael, you're an atheist!" (I can just hear that good old southern "twang" as he said "Michael".) Mike told me that he would feel most indignant, explaining his good Catholic roots to his sponsor and the fact that he attended regular mass and confessions. His sponsor's retort is what hits home for me. He'd say, "Yeah, maybe, but you don't trust God."

Fear is that simple – we do not trust God! I found in my life, though, that overcoming it is *not* that simple. I also found that I had to fight each "fear battle" on its own; it was not a case of "one battle for all fears". This time with Step 4, though, for the first time in my life I had a definite plan of action that really worked, and this step also provided me with a structured framework to work within. A big lesson I learnt was patience. I have had many fears; some have been removed and some are being removed. I had a fear of alcohol, crowds, loneliness, boredom, homosexuals, financial insecurity and rejection, to name but a few. As I write now, all these fears have been removed, except for the fear of rejection. The fear of economic insecurity (powerlessness) took six-and-a-half years of patience before the Lord gave me victory over it, but that is something I will be going through in more detail in Step 12.

Herein lies the *truth* of my predicament: although I want to, I find it difficult to trust God. All the tough talk, the brave posture, and all the head knowledge falls to the wayside when, for example, I feel disrespected by my wife (rejection). Once again, I am faced with something that I am totally powerless over. No matter how hard I try to reason with myself and think logically, the feeling overwhelms me. Unfortunately, I react in a very "un-user-friendly" manner. My response to the feeling of being rejected is to become angry. As I've mentioned before, I have a mouth like a sewer at times, and people get very hurt and offended by my outbursts – and I can't say I blame them; it is socially unacceptable behaviour.

My eyes were opened to the idea that anger can be a response to fear through my dog (God works in mysterious ways sometimes!). I had a little Scottish terrier called George. I got him about eight months after I had finished working the Program. He had already been named when I got him, and I asked why the name George. I was told it was because the then president of the USA, George Bush, had a little black Scottie . . . Okay, I've drifted off the topic, but I thought that was an interesting story! As part of my dog's training, I used to use a rolled-up newspaper. When I tapped him on the backside, it made a loud noise but didn't hurt. As he got out of the puppy stage, he started cocking his leg on the furniture instead of going outside to relieve himself. I would catch him by his collar, rub his nose in it and tap his backside with the newspaper. Instead of yelping, he would growl and try to bite me. I knew he was afraid because he would wet the floor while trying to bite. I realized that it was the nature of a Scottish terrier to react to fear in this way. A Yorkshire terrier or Cocker Spaniel I found quite the opposite; they yelp and cower and shiver, sometimes for a long time afterwards. This is their nature. I have come to realize that, in the same way, we humans react differently to fear from one person to another.

Some of our fears stem from our human instinct for survival, as well as from our nature that empathizes or sympathizes with others or loved ones in various scenarios. I believe that these natural instincts for survival and realistic concerns often mutate for various reasons,[34] and

---

34. These reasons can include, but are not limited to: unhealthy obsessions, lack of trust in God through lack of time spent in His presence, lack of understanding and belief through not spending enough time reading the Bible, the influence of the devil by listening to the lying thoughts he puts in our minds, outside influences like television and media that fill our minds with disproportionate truths, and so on . . .

this leaves an unhealthy trust or lack of trust for things that we know deep down to be fallible; things we should never place our trust in from the beginning. I need to emphasize that my response to fear, and indeed fear itself, is a sin and not condonable at all. Chad, one of my old pastors from the coast, used to like mentioning that our response is our responsibility; that we can be right, but wrong at the top of our voices. I often owe my wife an apology for my response to the fear of rejection, for instance. My feelings and fears of rejection have nothing to do with her. Her behaviour may be a catalyst, but if that was removed, something else would bring up that fear and my subsequent reactive response; it's what's inside me that comes out, not what anyone is doing.

But those things which proceed out of the mouth come forth from the heart; and they defile the man.

Matthew 15:18

If we want to be rid of fear, I believe we need to take ownership and responsibility for it. We then need to acknowledge it as sin, because God commands us to not fear and, quite simply, if we do fear, we do not trust Him. The command not to fear, and the many variants of this commandment in the Bible, make it one of the commandments given most often by God. By not trusting God, most of us put our trust in something else, even if we do so unconsciously, and this can very often be self-reliance. I have found it vitally important in my relationship with God to be deadly honest about my sin, which in this case is fear. I believe sin that we try to keep hidden in darkness, enables Satan to twist things and work it into something even more evil and difficult to get rid of, because

159

it grows and mutates. Darkness is the devil's stomping ground, but if we bring sin into the light, he can't mess with us anymore. Also, don't forget to persevere, even if you feel you keep bringing the same fear back to God on a daily basis. As long as you are sincere, He'll forgive you every time until *He* eventually removes it from your life.

I have come to realize that fear expressed in various forms, is generally rooted in only a few main fears. As I have mentioned before, I believe the expression of these root fears can vary in each person, but they all point to only a few main ones. Although fears are really another book on their own, I would like to touch briefly on a few of the root fears I have come across in my life. I am not suggesting that these root fears are exhaustive, but for me they are the ones that I find all my other fears seem to link back to. What I have found by viewing the root fears in my Fears Inventory, is that it gave me a feeling that overcoming them may not be as daunting as I originally thought, and this helped me remain willing to persevere with the Program. Still, the most important breakthrough in these root-cause fears is that I can clearly see that they exist only because I do not trust God.

The four root fears I am briefly going to outline are the fears of ceasing to exist, physical harm, powerlessness and rejection. I found that the fear of ceasing to exist included the fear of the unknown, so I was essentially fearful of the change to my current state of existence. I know that there is life after death, but what if I don't make the grade? Fear of death is also included in this, which is why I had a fear of drowning. I'm sure everyone can think of their own "death-fear". Fear of physical harm includes a lot of the physical fears: spiders, animals, mutilation of body parts, aggressive people, medical procedures, and that sort of thing. This fear is the thought of trying to live and/or adapt to a life where we are disfigured or altered in such a way that our normal way of living will have to be changed; we fear we may lose something we have and will not be able to cope. The fear that comes through the feeling of powerlessness is that awful feeling – like you're not in control. I could never handle a roller coaster because of this reason. I disliked situations where I did not know what was going to happen, and I have never liked surprises. Many social interactions create that feeling of powerlessness and include things as severe as abuse or rape. Many of us feel restricted or trapped, and quite claustrophobic. However, fear of rejection is the one that I battle with the most, and I believe it is the one that does the most damage in the world. That fear of being abandoned or not wanted can be mentally damaging. I really battle getting the silent treatment from someone because of this,[35] and sometimes I think I'd prefer it if someone had a go at me rather than ignore me. Very often fear of humiliation or being made a fool of in public is linked to rejection as well. The underlying thought that people may not see us in the light we think we are portraying ourselves in, can be quite scary for some. The interesting thing is that these are all our own perceptions, and I personally think that very few people view us in the light of how we are wanting to present ourselves. Vossie, who is one of my friends and mentors, often uses an old

---

35. I am very glad the Bible says in Ephesians 4:26-27, *"Be ye angry, and sin not; let not the sun go down on your wrath: Neither give place to the devil"*, as my wife and I try to live by this, and it has a positive impact on our relationship.

saying, "If I get your approval, that's fine; but if I don't, I will survive without it." The truth is that it is God's approval that ultimately counts, not man's.

If we can get to a place where we are trusting in God, we will know that we will be with Him forever in paradise (no need to fear not existing), and that no harm will befall us that He is incapable of leading us through and restoring to us one day (need not fear physical harm). We are not powerless if Christ is our strength, and we are not rejected, because as His children He will never leave us or forsake us. The only way we will be able to have the strength to overcome our fears is if God gives us the power to do so, and this is what we are doing here. I believe that the Lord will remove each of our fears in His own time, and we will discuss this further in Step 7.

As mentioned, I believe that fear is a sin because it shows we don't trust God, and this destroys our relationship with Him. I therefore need to make a note to make restitution to God through prayer and meditation.

The action for Step 4's fears

Fears Inventory

Download the Fears Inventory worksheet,[36] or draw up a blank template on a piece of paper from my example on page 165. Make as many copies as you need.

Follow and read quickly through my personal example of the Fears Inventory example and worksheet on pages 163

---

36. https://www.malcolmdown.co.uk/worksheets

to 165. As you go through each stage and complete each column, you can refer back to this example. Once again, you will not need to write down your reasonings, as I have done, you need only fill in the worksheets. As with the resentments, there is also a prompt sheet for fears on page 166, which you can use to help remember hidden fears you may not have remembered.

How I filled in the first fear

Column

1. Spiders

2. I've heard of spider bites and what they can do to people if the spider is poisonous enough, but I've never actually been bitten. I have seen pictures of bites that have rotted the flesh away. I come over cold and sweaty when I see spiders on the nature programmes on television. I had an experience in the bushveld, where I was doing a conservation practical on random animal counts, and I went under a low thorn tree. I walked into a thick neon-yellow spider web, which pulled this neon-blue spider onto my face; it was about the size of my palm. It ran off my face, down my neck and onto my shoulder, where I was able to flick it off. I was finished! I went cold and felt faint. I had nightmares for years afterwards. My logic tells me that nothing will really happen, but I cannot deal with it.

3. This fear stems from my natural instincts of self-preservation, which I believe have mutated into an unhealthy fear obsession of physical harm.

4. As I start to pray and ask God for His help in overcoming this fear that is rooted in the fear of physical harm, I realize that spiders are one of God's creations and that I really do not trust Him much if I think that He could not protect me from a little spider. I need to prepare myself to have Him remove this fear as I wait on Him. It may seem an insignificant fear, but I found that I was not able to overcome it on my own.

Personal Example of My Fears Inventory Worksheet

	1. The fear	2. The reason or cause	3. The nature or root cause	4. Future action
	I am fearful of . . .	I am fearful because . . .	This fear stems from . . .	I will . . .pray and ask God for His strength
1.	Spiders	Their creepiness, speed, they bite and could have poison	Physical harm	Pray and ask God
2.	Being ignored or humiliated	I am scared when I think that people will ignore me or laugh at me	Rejection	Pray and ask God
3.	Abandonment	I am scared that those I love too much might one day just up and leave me	Rejection	Pray and ask God
4.	Hell	I am scared I don't "make the grade" and end up in hell for eternity one day	Extinction	Pray and ask God

Fears Inventory Worksheet Prompts

Fear of . . .

Writing an inventory
Rejection
Alcohol
Sex
Authority
Employment
Insects
Doctors/dentists
Being found out
Success
Fear itself
Women
Crying
The unknown
Disapproval
Hospitals
Hurting others
Being alive
Gossip
Change

Dying
Loneliness
Drugs
Sin
Heights
Parents
Losing a child
Police
Stealing
Gays and lesbians
Responsibility
Drowning
People
Poverty
Abandonment
Confrontation
Feelings
Violence
Government
Wealthy people

Insanity
Diseases
Relapse
Self-expression
Unemployment
Losing a spouse
Animals
Jail
Creditors
Failure
Physical pain
Men
Being alone
Races
Intimacy
Sobriety
Getting old
God
Gangs
Guns

You might have others that spring to mind because these have triggered a memory. Put them on your Fears Inventory worksheet.

Practical steps for fears

1) Get your Fears Inventory worksheet out next to you with a pencil. In this inventory your character defect is fear itself – you don't trust God. Your amends will be made with God only. Write down *all* your fears under column 1 ("I am fearful of . . .") without doing anything to the other columns. Your fears must include past fears, which you feel you don't have anymore; they might actually still be there but are not currently activated. I suggest that you write down all those that come to mind now; pray and ask God to reveal them to you.

2) After you have written down all the fears you can think of, read through the Fears Inventory Worksheet Prompts on page 166, filling in on your worksheet all fears that then spring to mind under the first column. This will obviously continue on from the fears you have already listed from memory.

Now you need to complete columns 2–4 for each point, working across columns 2–4 one at a time, and then going onto the next until all are complete . . .

3) Write down the cause or reason of your fear in column 2. If you look at the example on page 163, I gave my explanation of arachnophobia so that you can see that no fear is too stupid. (I'm a 6.3ft tall fella, weighing around 20 stone, and my little wife has to protect me!)

   Follow the explanation of my reasoning and do your own for each of your fears as you go. I suggest actually trying to relive them in your mind and then put in a brief line to sum up the reasoning, which will help you recall or remember it again for later.

4) Ask the Lord to reveal to you where this fear is rooted; is it the fear of Ceasing to Exist, Physical Harm, Powerlessness or Rejection? Write down which you feel it is. If you are as sincere as you can be, you can count on it being the one God has revealed to you. If you believe in another root-cause fear and would prefer to use that one, please feel free to do so, using the same method explained in this section.

5) Fill in for each of the fourth column spaces, <u>Pray and ask God</u> (underline each), as you make up your mind that you would like to be rid of each fear. I need to want God to remove this fear, because I want to have a close relationship with Him – this will be for future action in Step 7. You have now completed your Fears Inventory.

Harms or hurt

Harms are wrong acts which result in pain, hurt feelings, worry, financial loss, etc. – this includes towards yourself.

The harms we look at would more than likely have been done to people or institutions, and this makes it easier to go off of our Resentments worksheet, because we have already listed them there. It does not mean we would have harmed everyone we had a resentment towards, but I think that quite a few of the harms we have done will already be on our resentment list.

When it comes to dealing with harms, I found that I had to ask for God to open my eyes. As a child growing up, and even as an "adult" for that matter, I never saw myself as one harming others, but rather as the one being harmed. One gift I am very grateful for, which I believe the Lord graced me with from birth, is that I am not really a vindictive person. My heart goes out in compassion to people who suffer with bitter vindictiveness, because I believe it holds them in bondage a long time. It's not their fault, and many times they really have been aggrieved. I have found that we need to be rid of it, so keep on *willing* God to remove it through prayer. In most of my conflicts and disagreements where I may have actually been hurt or hard done by, I simply wanted nothing more to do with the person. I never wished them any ill or blessing, nor felt joy or jealousy at either their failure or success; I just totally cut them off. Cutting them off was not right, although I will say I never compounded the problem by interfering with the other person or their life. In as much as the bridge might have been damaged, it wasn't "burnt", so to speak. This meant that in my resentment towards someone for something they might have done to me, I very seldom did anything disrespectful towards them. In other words, I did not harm them. I did harm my relationship with God, though, and, of course, myself.

When I was studying (not philosophy) I came up with a philosophy that as long as I did not intentionally hurt somebody, I was in the right and therefore a good person. I have come to understand that this philosophy was nonsense, to put it mildly. It meant that I never had to try to get along with or try to understand anyone. It got me into a lot of hot water over the years as I stepped callously on people's toes and didn't care. Most of the harms and hurts I created in others' lives were out of total inconsideration. I used to say the most inappropriate things at the most inappropriate times, and this used to hugely offend people.

I was once at a student friend's twenty-first birthday celebration in Pietermaritzburg. His mother had bought a pig, which was on the rotisserie in the garden – head 'n' all. I was drunk (no excuse) and got all on my high horse about this pig's head. I stood watching the eyeballs sizzling, which I found disgusting, and blurted out as much. I moaned very loudly about how I could not believe someone would do such a thing and not cut the head off at least. Apparently, the mother was highly upset and embarrassed, because it had cost her a large sum of money and she had done her best. Some of the other people there got irate with me and told me to leave. I thought I was fully within my "liberal" right to have voiced my opinion.

There was an occasion in a restaurant where I complained about the food and the service. My wife had asked that I let it go because she felt embarrassed about me making a scene. I did not consider her feelings at all and proceeded to carry on and have the manager come over. He eventually apologised and I got a new plate of food, but the evening was not the same after that.

When I was an adolescent, there was this time that I did do a "planned harm" to a nasty schoolteacher. To be fair, though, I did it more because it was naughty than because I was acting on a malicious grudge. My friend and I used to walk home after school when we lived in Ladysmith. I must have been about thirteen years old, and our route home took us past the school hostels. This particular teacher used to park his car in the fenced-off parking lot of the hostel grounds during the day, and our footpath took us right along the fence. We got ourselves syringes filled with brake fluid and sprayed it through the fence onto his car's bonnet. Of course, the brake fluid ate the paint and discoloured the bonnet. There were big announcements and inquiries made at school the following day, but it was difficult for them to know who it was, and we were never caught.

It sounds funny now, but those people were really hurt. Most hurts occurred through what I said. I could say some really hurtful things, especially when drunk.

I believe it is important to list all sexual activity outside of the bonds of marriage between a husband and wife as a harm. The Word of God is very clear on the strength of bond that forms between a man and a woman that are intimate on a sexual level (Genesis 2:21-24). This is God's design.

> He replied, "Have you never read that He who created them from the beginning made them male and female, and said, 'For this reason a man shall leave his father and mother and shall be joined inseparably to his wife, and the two shall become one flesh'? So they are no longer two, but one flesh. Therefore, what God has joined together, let no one separate."
>
> Matthew 19:4-6 (AMP)

I went into these harms having heard this scripture but not having paid too much attention to it. At the time, I am sorry to say, I was only interested in fulfilling my desire or want. If the woman happened to enjoy it then lucky for her, and it was an added boost to my already inflated ego. I now believe that by creating this bond, I was causing harm to any relationships or marriage she may have in the future, as well as doing damage to mine as well. That is why I believe it is vitally important to get these all down on paper.

In our harms, we need to include ourselves. I have unwittingly inflicted all these hurts and afflictions that others experience onto myself as well.

We need to view the harms in the same way we reviewed our resentments. We start by putting down in one sentence how we actually harmed the person. We then need to see the very defective nature of our harms: where was I selfish, self-seeking, dishonest, afraid and inconsiderate? And as always, I harm the Lord God more than anyone else, so I need to make a note to make amends to Him through prayer.

The action for Step 4's harms or hurts

Harms and Hurts Inventory

Download the Harms Inventory worksheet[37] or draw up a blank template on a piece of paper from my example on page 175. Follow and read quickly through my personal example of the Harms Inventory example and worksheet on pages 173 to 175. As you go through each stage and complete each column, you can refer back to this example. As before, you will not need to write down your reasoning for each as I have done; just fill in the worksheets.

---

37. https://www.malcolmdown.co.uk/worksheets

How I filled in my fourth harm on my list

Column

1. Bricklayer

2. I bad-mouthed his name to other contractors. It harmed him because in the construction industry, soiling another man's reputation can leave him without work and bankrupt. It is one thing to be asked about the quality of an artisan's work and be honest, but quite another thing when you make it your mission to "get the guy"; I believe that you are then playing God. I know that he lost work because of my explicit intention of hurting him.

3. Was I . . .

   - *Selfish?* – yes, because I had not thought of the difficulties he might be experiencing (I put down Selfish and underline it).

   - *Self-seeking?* – yes, I wanted the work done exactly my way with no room for any deviation (I put down Self-seeking and underline it).

   - *Dishonest?* – yes, I made him seem much worse than he probably was. I used statements like, "He's the worst bricklayer I've ever worked with" (I put down Dishonest and underline it).

   - *Frightened?* – no, because I didn't care what he said or thought; I never even thought about his reaction.

- *Inconsiderate?* – yes, because I never considered any scenario as to why he couldn't keep up with the building programme. If I think about it now, he could have had labour issues, transport problems, personal hassles at home; I never bothered to ask or listen
(I put <u>Inconsiderate</u> and underline it).

4. As it is a harm I have done, I will want to make amends to God, which will restore my relationship with Him. I am willing to make amends with the person harmed, which will either restore my relationship with them, or at least clear my side of the street. That is why I will always put <u>Prayer</u> and <u>Amends</u> under harms and underline it.

Personal Example of My Harms Inventory Worksheet (Sexual and Non-sexual)

	1. The harm	2. How I harmed	3. My part that caused the harm	4. Future action
	Whom did I harm? I harmed . . .	What did I do? I . . .	Was I . . . selfish, self-seeking, dishonest, frightened, or inconsiderate?	I will . . . pray and make amends
1.	My mum	Swore at her, heaped guilt and blame on her	Selfish, self-seeking, dishonest, frightened and inconsiderate	Prayer and amends
2.	Ex-girlfriend	Slept with her, with no thought of her feelings or future	Selfish, self-seeking and inconsiderate	Prayer and amends
3.	Old school	Threw rocks through as many windows as possible	Selfish, dishonest and inconsiderate	Prayer and amends
4.	Bricklayer	Bad-mouthed his name to all other contractors	Selfish, self-seeking, dishonest, and inconsiderate	Prayer and amends

Practical steps for harms and hurts

1) Get your Harms Inventory worksheet out next to you with a pencil. Write down all your harms under the first column ("I harmed . . .") that come to mind now, without doing anything to the other columns.

2) After you have written all the harms you can think of, go back to your Resentments Inventory worksheet which you previously completed. Go through each resentment and ask yourself if you may have harmed any of these people or institutions in any way. It might be physically, verbally, or even through silence (not speaking up and protecting the innocence of whomever I have a resentment towards). Write down what you did or how you harmed that person or institution in the second column ("I . . ."), without doing anything in the other columns. Just put a brief summary of what you actually did, so that you'll be able to recall the situation in full in Step 5.

Now you need to complete columns 3 and 4 for each point.

3) Start with column 3 and ask what part of your character defects caused you to do the harm or hurt. Then, as shown in the example, write down whether you were selfish, self-seeking, dishonest, frightened or inconsiderate; then underline each one.

4) By filling in column 4, we are only making our work easier for Steps 8 and 9. You are not going to do anything here; you are merely displaying willingness to "clean your side of the street". In dealing with a harm, no matter the justification of

what you did to the person or institution (as put down in column 2), you wronged them. We need to be willing to make an amends to God through prayer and to that person or institution through an amends (remember, it might be with no actual contact). Once you are willing, put <u>Prayer</u> and <u>Amends</u> in column 4, and <u>underline</u> them.

That is the Harms Inventory worksheet completed.

Good Qualities

I would like to discuss another aspect of our moral inventory which often eludes us because it hides under the auspices of being our good qualities. What makes it even more subtle is that very often we receive high praise and accolades from other people for these so-called good qualities, as they can have such a positive effect on and for others. The aspect of our good qualities that I am going to talk about here is our true motive behind what we do – the heart.

As human beings we are very result oriented. We often praise people who have succeeded in gaining power, wealth, a following, a husband or wife, etc. From successful people we also want to see evidence of philanthropy (charitable deeds): is he helping the poor, is he being kind to children, does he love animals . . .? Such a person is often considered to have really good qualities. The true motive for someone "doing-good" can, however, actually be wrong. With celebrities, for instance, you may find charitable acts and deeds that are used for marketing and exposure, while we watch on impressed with what they are doing for others (I am not going to give examples so that I avoid hurting anyone, but I'm sure you can think of many examples in the world).

In order to see just how subtle people's motives can be, read the story of the prodigal son in Luke 15:11-32. The end of the story is here below:

> But the elder brother became angry and deeply resentful and was not willing to go in; and his father came out and began pleading with him. But he said to his father, "Look! These many years I have served you, and I have never neglected or disobeyed your command. Yet you have never given me [so much as] a young goat, so that I might celebrate with my friends; but when this [other] son of yours arrived, who has devoured your estate with immoral women, you slaughtered that fattened calf for him!" The father said to him, "Son, you are always with me, and all that is mine is yours. But it was fitting to celebrate and rejoice, for this brother of yours was [as good as] dead and has begun to live. He was lost and has been found."   Luke 15:28-32 (AMP)

What I want to focus on in this parable is the older son. On the surface he appears very honest, loyal and hardworking, but note his reaction when he hears that his brother is back and his father has taken him in with a robe, a ring and a feast. He tries to use the old "martyr routine" about what's fair. He's not interested in his father's well-being or happiness; he's worried that what he's expecting to inherit from his father one day is being depleted. You see, he wants his father's things, just like his younger brother had, only he's "being good" in order to get them. His heart is purely self-centred, and this is what makes it wrong, as God looks at the heart and not at the outward.

When I was still in school I can remember going to school with a packet of sweets I'd got for my birthday. I opened the packet on the playground and let all the kids take one; I wouldn't even have one myself. The kids thanked me and mentioned what a sharing chap I was. Actually, the reason I made this sacrifice was to be liked by the other kids, not to bring joy and happiness to them. The fact that it did bring them some joy and happiness was a by-product or an added bonus. My motive was purely self-centred.

The irony is that in both these stories, the one who looked "good" lost out. The eldest son never went into the feast and probably never received his full inheritance; and the next day at school the kids went back to what I felt was ignoring me again. If our motives had been right, we would have got some enjoyment and no heartache or disappointment, regardless of the others' responses.

God is not impressed by results or outward appearances. He looks at our heart.

For the LORD seeth not as man seeth; for man looketh on the outward appearance, but the LORD looketh on the heart.   1 Samuel 16:7

Perhaps surprisingly, a good heart does not always produce a good outward result. There is that story of a little old granny standing on the side of the road hunched over her walking stick, facing the traffic going by. A young man walks by and decides to help the poor old lady across the busy road. He is on his own and his only motive is that he feels compassion for someone in need. Greeting her cheerfully, he announces his assistance and whisks her briskly across the road by her arm. When they stop at the other side, she tries to swat him with her handbag as she shrieks, "What are you doing, you naughty man? I was waiting for my bus, and there it goes!"

I was coming out of a pub one evening many years ago, in a jovial mood. I walked to the car park and saw a man hitting a woman. She was screaming and crying as he held onto her hair, punching at her face. I rushed over and wrenched him off, and then proceeded to rough him up a bit. The woman rushed up and jumped onto my back and started clawing at my face and trying to bite me. She was screaming even more than before for me to leave her poor husband alone. I had had no intention of gaining anything, I was just trying to help someone being assaulted. They walked off to their car in each other's arms, and I was left feeling rather silly and perplexed!

I suspect that this kind of outcome is rare – the exception to the rule – and I'm sure our heavenly Father enjoys the humorous side to our attempts. If your motive is in any way for your own benefit, you are probably on the wrong path. If it is for others or, better still, for God, you are on the right track.

Please understand that I'm not talking about going to the extreme of sacrifice where you end up being a martyr or a doormat; you do need to look after yourself as well. What use would you be to anyone if you were ill or dead? The point is that your heart (motive) needs to be one of pleasing God and helping others, not for self-gain.

The action for Step 4's good qualities

Good Qualities Inventory

Download the Good Qualities Inventory worksheet[38] or draw up a blank template on a piece of paper from my example on page 183.

Follow and read quickly through my personal example and worksheet of the Good Qualities Inventory on pages 181 to 183. As you go through each stage and complete each column, you can refer back to this example. As before, you will not need to write down your reasoning as I have done, only to fill in the worksheets.

How I filled in the third good quality

Column

1. Comical

2. I have always had a good sense of humour, and I used to like telling myself that it is because I liked to make people laugh. But after analysing the situation properly, I realized that when people didn't find me funny or ignored me, I used to feel incredibly hurt and upset. This allowed me to understand that I was only seeking attention and had little or no regard for other people's well-being or happiness.

3. My true motive is the "Wrong" moral standard. As I've said, any motive that is primarily for the benefit of *self* is wrong. The ultimate motive is

---

38. https://www.malcolmdown.co.uk/worksheets

out of love for God, but if we are wanting to help or benefit someone else, we are showing God's love to others, and this pleases Him. However, my primary concern was for my interests and feeding my own ego. I was self-seeking, not really interested in whether others were happy or not.

4.   I will pray and ask God to change my motive, so I put Pray and ask God for help in the column and underline it. I will ask God for forgiveness for my self-seeking motive and ask Him to instil a new moral standard in my life; one where I do things for the benefit of others, so that ultimately His glory might shine. I realize this will not necessarily change overnight, so I will continue to pray this prayer until there is a genuine change.

Personal Example of My Good Qualities Inventory Worksheet

1. The good quality	2. Motive	3. Quality of the motive	4. Future action
What are my good qualities? I am . . .	What is my reason? I am . . ., because . . .	What was my moral standard in this motive? Right or Wrong	I will . . . pray and ask for help, or pray and thank God
1. Honest	I am Honest because I am scared of being caught and looking stupid	Wrong – Self-conscious	Pray and ask God for help
2. Fair	I am fair because I want them to be fair to me in return	Wrong – Self-interest	Pray and ask God for help
3. Comical	I am comical because I want people to like me and focus attention on me	Wrong – Self-seeking	Pray and ask God for help
4. Punctual	I am punctual because I know how it feels to have to wait for someone	Right – Considerate	Pray and thank God
5. Methodical	I am methodical because I don't want others to struggle later if I had not done it right first time	Right – Helpful	Pray and thank God

Practical steps for good qualities

1) Get your Good Qualities Inventory worksheet out next to you with a pencil. Write down all your good qualities you can think of under the first column ("I am . . .") without doing anything to the other columns.

   I suggest that you write down all those that come to mind now.

   Give yourself free reign and try to think of things that others compliment you on, and also things that you think people don't recognize. You can also put down natural abilities if you feel that they are qualities that might benefit others. You might, for instance, be a good football player and you know this pleases your father; put it down. Think also of attitudes towards things that might inspire others to do better. For instance, a passionate approach to your work that gets your colleagues inspired and performing well. Remember that we are going to review motives, so don't think you are boasting by putting things down; we need an honest appraisal of how we see ourselves. Look at the few examples I have put down on the worksheet on page 183 to give you a guide. I have tried to pick a variety of good qualities from my personal inventory, which I did back then.

2) You will need to be rigorously honest when filling in column 2. I suggest you do as I did, praying and asking God to open your eyes to your true motives. Remember, no one need see this part of your

inventory – ever. This is between you and God. If you really would like your good qualities to have pure and true motives, you need to get honest with yourself and God. This is what I did, and I can tell you that these days I am more honest because I know that this pleases the Lord, and I believe that my motive has changed over time by God's power and grace; I didn't have to fight it. Write down your true motive for your good quality under the second column ("I am [put the good quality down], because [put your motive down]") without doing anything to the other columns.

Now complete column 3 and 4 together for each good quality to the end, and then do that for each one down your list.

3) When doing column 3, it is quite easy to determine a right or wrong motive. If the concern is primarily for your benefit, it's wrong. If your main concern is for the well-being of others or to please the Lord, your motive is right. Try, as I have in my example, to put why you think your motive was wrong or right; it can just be one word. I have found that it has helped me gain more perspective, but it is not a necessity; I had a few right or wrong motives that I couldn't find a word to explain.

4) The fourth column is much like the other inventories when it comes to praying; we will be asking God to change our wrong motives. In column 4 you would put Prayer and ask God for help (underline it) for where you marked "Wrong" in column 3. I also think it is important in the process of recovery

to thank and praise God for the goodness He has placed in us where our motive was pure. In column 4 you will put <u>Prayer</u> and <u>thanks</u> (underline it) for where you had marked "Right" in column 3. Before the foundations of the earth were created, God had already given us these good qualities, and it is a privilege to show Him gratitude for helping us to keep our motives pure in all we've been through; not through our power, but through His.

You have now completed Step 4. Well done! I promise you it is already having a huge impact on your life.

Step 5

We admitted to God though Jesus Christ, to ourselves and to another human being, the exact nature of our wrongs.

(Confession)

Confess your faults one to another, and pray one for another, that ye may be healed. The effectual fervent prayer of a righteous man availeth much. James 5:16

"Rory, how free do you want to be?"

This was a question my mentor asked me over and over during my inventory, and it is my question to you too. I was privileged to have a mentor to go through Step 4 with me the second time, but the first time I did it on my own, with a couple of pointers from a different sponsor. When the time came for Step 5, I did not know which "human being" to pick to share "the exact nature of [my] wrongs" with. Choosing the right person to do Step 5 with is very important and, even then, there were some things I felt I just could not bring myself to share with them.

I think we first need to understand why it is so important to have to admit to ourselves, to God and to another human being the exact nature of our wrongs. By writing everything down in Step 4 I have essentially admitted them to myself, I might just need to read through them again. I think I knew most of my wrongs anyway, but the inventory helped me to put them into perspective and identify their actual nature – in other words what the root cause was.

When interacting with God, I believe He wants us to communicate openly with Him, even if we recognize the fact that He knows everything already. I think this is important, because if we read and think about this scripture:

> *If thou shalt confess with thy mouth the Lord Jesus, and shalt believe in thine heart that God hath raised him from the dead, thou shalt be saved.* Romans 10:9

Why would He want us to confess with our mouth to Him when He is omniscient (all-knowing)? There are two reasons, I believe.

The first is that we as humans tend to quickly put things out of our minds when we don't really want to think about them. Truth be told, we *know* that God knows everything, but we do not want Him to know our wrongs; we want Him to think we are better than we really are. If we are not sitting down and actually confessing our wrongs out loud to God, we have a remarkable tendency to squash them down into our subconscious and forget about them. In this way, I think humans are very much like the myth about ostriches with their heads buried in the sand: as long as we can't see something, then it is surely not there! If we make ourselves consciously aware of the fact that God sees our defects of character, there is a certain amount of godly fear in us, and this is a huge motivator for us to really want to change. For me, there was also a bit of shame in the fact that I disappoint God so often, even though I really do not want to.

The way I see it, the second reason involves Satan himself, and I believe it has to do with the very fact that he is *not* omniscient. The devil trembles at the thought of God, and when he knows that you are open with the Lord about your wrongs, it is far more difficult for him to use lies on you. I think it is sad, and I very much include myself in this statement, that the devil understands with greater comprehension than we do, the immense power and authority residing in us by the Holy Spirit. He knows this power is far greater than himself, and that he *has* to submit to it. What an amazing thing it would be if we believed it as much, and actually stood on that authority we have in Jesus.

I recall a time when I was a kid playing at home and I accidently broke a window. I was scared to tell my dad and thought it would be better to say nothing and "play dumb" if he asked me what had happened to the window. The problem was that my friend from next door saw me break the window, and he very lovingly reminded me of the trouble I'd be in if my father knew it was me who had broken it. "You'd get into real big trouble if you tell him," he assured me. I realized my "friend" would have one over me if I lied to my dad, and that I would pretty much have to be at his beck and call in order to keep him from telling my dad the truth. With this in mind, I plucked up courage that evening and told my dad the truth, and he was surprisingly proud of the fact that I was honest. My father forgave me and got the window fixed. The next day the lad who'd seen me break the window started taunting me, but he could not scare or threaten me at all, because he had no power; my dad already knew about it, and it was okay. I believe it works the same with God and the devil. It is important to know that, unlike God, the devil cannot read your thoughts. This is why I believe it is so important to confess aloud. When the devil hears you confessing your iniquities to God, he tends to leave you alone, as he knows that Jesus' death on the cross has long ago paid for that sin.

Another thing I discovered is that when I confessed my sins, the guilt vanished, and I felt a certain level of peace.

When it comes to sharing the exact nature of our wrongs with another human being, we really need to know why we have to do that. After all, if God knows, what has it got to do with anyone else? This part is probably one of the most crucial aspects leading to the success of the Program.

The first benefit comes from a certain amount of accountability. Although he is not your boss and you owe him nothing, having someone ask you how it is going from time to time keeps those things fresh in your mind. This stops us from pushing our wrongs back down inside us as easily. For me, one of the biggest reliefs I had was the fact that somebody knew about *all* my wrongs, and all was okay. *It was OK!* I never lost my job, my dignity, my reputation, my life, etc.; it was okay. What an amazing weight off my shoulders. I could walk up straight, look the world in the eye and know it was all okay. This does not mean that you won't lose any of the things I mentioned, but I believe you will still feel a weight taken off – those things are replaceable, and God has things in store for you that are more in line with the plans He has for you.

I feel one needs to reveal *everything*. If you know there is something you can never tell, that is the thing you must be *willing* to tell. As I said before though, if you have a sincere desire to be straight and honest, but you cannot be at present, do not be discouraged; it will come. Show your commitment by telling the person everything you can and mention that there is something you are not ready to speak about. God sees your honesty and He will work in your heart.

The person you choose to share the exact nature of your wrongs with can, in theory, be anyone. If you have a mentor or sponsor, they are usually a good choice. However, you might feel that there are things that you somehow know they will not be able to handle objectively. This was the case with one of my sponsors. As much as he helped me, he had a religious belief and a cultural stance which I believe would have prevented him from staying open and objective towards me once I'd shared some specific wrongs with him.

The person whom I was most afraid to tell was my mother, and for some reason she was the one I blurted my Step 5 to the first time. I knew I wanted to tell someone, just so long as I knew it was the right person. I prayed and asked God to present someone to me, telling Him I was willing and ready. Little did I know it would be my mother! I had gone to visit her one day, probably about six months into my sobriety, with no intention of doing my Step 5 with her. While we were talking, I had a sense of peace, and it all came out. She hugged me and said she was so glad we could have an open relationship once more. She never said anything else, and this is important too. We are not looking for advice or help, just a listening ear.

This is why it is so good to ask God to bring someone across your path (*Your will, God, not mine*). But remember you must be totally willing, with enough self-honesty to know you are not trying to procrastinate, otherwise when God does bring the right person along, you may overlook them. Other types of people you may choose are doctors, lawyers, clergy, counsellors, close friends or even a total stranger. Just remain willing and alert, and the Lord will bring the right person along.

Because my answer to the question at the beginning of Step 5 was "Very free" I had to "let it all hang out". There were always two things from way back in my life that I never wanted to ever get out but, somehow, I managed to share them. I have felt nervous to share them here in this book and had to ask my wife if I could. We never share things that might hurt or injure another, including their reputation or credibility. The world can be a harsh and judgemental place. There are many people who battle with similar scenarios to mine, and if you can relate to either of these situations, I believe the Lord wants you to know it is also *OK*.

One night I was driving back home drunk; I mean I was *seriously* inebriated. My speech was a slur, and I could not walk straight. I was driving at about 25 mph, and I came to a sharpish left bend in the road. It was a double-lane road in my direction, and I was in the left lane, which is the slow lane. There was a hidden entry road on the left bend and a car was indicating to turn right. In my drunken state,

I decided to stop and let the guy turn across me. This was inappropriate considering that the traffic was light in the evenings. The car just waited for me, so I stuck my arm out and waved him on. I guess he thought this was all rather crazy but didn't want to sit there all night, so he went across me. It must have been a combination of my lights shining at him and the fact that he couldn't see around the bend properly, but neither of us saw the minibus taxi come past me in the right lane. The taxi hit the driver's door of the other car at what must have been about 50 mph. The car spun around and bashed up against the curb. I noticed the minibus taxi had passengers in it as it veered across the road over the curb on the other side and smashed into a solid brick wall of a church. There was no movement from either vehicle, and I first thought of calling the ambulance and then going to check if the people were okay. Then I wondered what would happen when the police arrived and found me in this state. What if someone in the car was "okay" and told them what I had done? I did the most despicably selfish thing ever and drove off. That incident haunted me for years, and the guilt ate at me often.

The other thing that I couldn't talk about was the fact that I had been sexually abused by older boys when I was six, nine and twelve years old. What made it particularly bad for me later on, I think, was that I can't remember being really hurt. In fact, it all seemed rather secretive at the time. I do, however, vaguely recall being slightly hurt on one or two occasions, and then it wasn't fun being in the "big boys" group anymore. I was sworn to secrecy, on pain of death of course, but they fortunately moved to another town at some stage.

My sexual outlook was very messed up and warped in later life. I could not forgive myself or talk about it because I believed I'd opened up to it willingly. I felt I was to blame. I used to think if I had been badly hurt, I could tell people and they would feel sympathy for me and not revulsion. Anyway, it was all too humiliating to deal with.

These were the things I shared with my mum. She said nothing, and I believe it was the best way she could have handled it. The good thing was that she never changed one bit towards me – it was okay.

By the time I was doing my Step 5 a second time, it wasn't any easier. This time I went for prayer and counselling on this and other things. I believe that if something of a similar nature has happened to you, you too will need deliverance and counselling. It is not your fault, but I believe that it is enough for the devil to get a foot in and create a stronghold in your life. Pray and seek guidance as to whom you can go and see. Ask the church counsellor or pastor. We want to clear the wreckage of our past. Take courage in knowing that you are not alone, and it is not as frightening as you may think.

I asked God for the courage to share all with another, and then I did it. It was really very liberating; what a load off my mind! I think what also helped was the fact that God helped me pick the right person to tell; one of my mentors the second time around.

Something else that is important to remember is our obedience to the Bible. The scripture that goes with this step has a condition to our recovery. It says we have to confess our sins (nature of our wrongs) to each other so that we can *be healed* (restored in relationship). I found I need not understand any more than this for the healing to come, I just need to obey.

When I was busy working through the Program, I understood nothing about what was going on, as I share it now. All I knew was that I was surrounded by a bunch of happy individuals who told me that they had found a relationship with God by working through the steps and following the Program as honestly, willingly and with as much open-mindedness as they could muster. That was good enough for me because I really wanted this. As I now write many years later, there is one thing that stands out more than others as to how the Program worked when all else had failed. It is that it brought about a certain humility in my life, especially when I did Step 5. I realized that God could not do anything for me while "self" was in the way. The only way I have ever been able to achieve a semblance of humility is by working through these steps; not perfectly, but to the best of my ability. Few things are more humbling than having to share your dirty laundry with another person. This is why I believe this step to be critical in recovery.

At this point it will be important to go back and make sure you have left nothing out. If there are some things that you do not have the courage to open up about, just hand them over to God every day and remain willing. Pray and ask Him to reveal anything He wants you to bring to light, those things which might have slipped your mind. If you have done this and you feel a peace about having done your best, you will be in a different place in your life right now. If you feel you are still far from where you want to be, look back on your life and take heart from the fact that you are not where you used to be. I believe the end is not the goal; the journey is.

The action for Step 5

1) Get out your Resentment, Fears, Harms and Good Qualities worksheets, which you completed in Step 4. Find a quiet, secluded spot and start to tell God everything aloud, using your worksheets as a guide. Tell Him all your resentments, and what the nature of your wrongs were for each; whether you were selfish, self-seeking, dishonest, afraid or inconsiderate. Do the same with your harms. Then pick up your Fears sheet and tell Him all the things you are fearful of, making sure to acknowledge that you know that they are wrongs because you were not trusting in Him. Finally, go through your Good Qualities worksheets and tell Him where your motives were wrong, and why they were wrong. Pray and ask God to forgive you all these points from all 4 worksheets where you have indicated prayer or amends in the final columns, and ask Him to restore His relationship with you.

2) When you have finished, pray and ask God to show you if you have forgotten something or left anything out. If you remember anything, write it down on the appropriate worksheet and work through it as in Step 4. You will more than likely remember other things over time. If so, put them in your lists and follow the same procedure as with all the rest.

3) Try to find the right person to do your Step 5 with. It is a good idea to have a third person present if the person you choose is of the opposite sex, or in cases that may lead to any kind of emotional bonding. Pray and ask God, and if you feel a peace, go for it.

4) Once you have found the person, explain to them that as part of a Program you are doing, you'd like for them to lend an ear. Schedule a definite time with them that will suit you both. I used to meet once a week on Tuesdays at 5.30am, before I started work. Explain to your listener that you are not sure how many hours it will take and ask if that is okay with them.

5) I suggest you sit with them privately and do the same as you did with God. When you mention each cause, try to relate the scenario (the "whole story") to the listener. For example, rather than saying you have resentment towards so-and-so because they bullied you, try to explain. Say something like, "I used to attend such-and-such a high school when I was twelve years old. I was in Grade 7 and there was this bloke in my class named Bob who came from out of town. He seemed to have this way about him that he was trying to prove himself. One day on the playground . . ." Do you see what I'm trying to get at? Especially, try to relate your *feelings* at the time; try to relive the moment of each resentment, fear or harm. This is why I suggested in Step 4 to write down a few key words that would trigger the memory again.

6) *Do not try to rush through this.* It is difficult at times, but you need to really try to give your listener the true picture. We call this "not skimping on the mortar". With a building, if you skimp on the mortar in between your bricks, you are making the walls weak, and the house can come tumbling down later on (I really relate to this, being in the building industry). As an example, my Step 5 took over ten hours to relate, but it was worth every second for the peace of mind I have today.

7) I am reluctant to make the following point, as so many of us look for a loophole to get out of doing this part of the step, but I also do not want you to become disheartened. If you have truly done all you can to find someone to do this step with to no avail, do not lose heart; you can proceed to Step 6. Only you will know if you have really tried. If you are deceiving yourself, I can almost guarantee you the Program will fail; it is your choice. Bear in mind this is only temporary; you must continue to pray and actively seek to find someone as soon as possible. If your heart is sincere, it will not hinder the process and you will eventually find somebody. When you do find someone, do this Step 5 straight away with them. It will not matter where you are in the Program; just stop the other work and finish this Step 5.

8) Because this step is so important, pray once more and ask God to reveal if there is anything you might have left out. If you feel a calm and peace about it, you are ready for Step 6.

Step 6

We were entirely ready to have God, through Jesus Christ, remove all these defects of character.

(Willingness)

If ye be willing and obedient, ye shall eat the good of the land. Isaiah 1:19

This Program is full of surprises, and Step 6 was no different for me. When asked if I was entirely ready to have God remove all my defects, I immediately answered, "Of course!", without really thinking – who wouldn't? I thought Step 6 would be easy and straightforward; after all, if I was able to hand over my drinking problem to God and He had removed it, this should be a walk in the park. In essence I guess it is, provided my attitude is right. This step has, however, proved to be one of the more difficult steps. Not because it takes time or a huge effort, but actually because it requires very little effort. This is harder to do than one thinks because it is natural for us to want to at least try *something*. Letting go totally and allowing God to guide you will require a miracle in itself.

I have come to realize that each battle in life has to be fought individually, and on its own merit. Some character flaws are easier than others and disappear quickly, mainly because we really want God to remove them, I think. Others take time because either we don't really want to let go of them, or we do not trust that God will act. It seems silly that we trust Him in some big areas of our lives, while in smaller areas we find it difficult. Whatever the reason is, I have found that the process of learning to trust and really hand over to God is what builds character and forges our relationship with Him. It is truly a beautiful thing if we sincerely follow through with it. Personally, I believe that our character is the thing that will determine what we do in eternity.

> Moreover [let us also be full of joy now!] let us exult and triumph in our troubles and rejoice in our sufferings, knowing that pressure and affliction and hardship produce patient and unswerving endurance. And endurance (fortitude) develops maturity of character (approved faith and tried integrity). And character [of this sort] produces [the habit of] joyful and confident hope of eternal salvation. Such hope never disappoints or deludes or shames us, for God's love has been poured out in our hearts through the Holy Spirit Who has been given to us.   Romans 5:3-5 (AMP)

I believe this to be the essence of our development. I chose The Amplified Bible here, because it gives a wonderful explanation of the word "character" ("approved faith and tried integrity"). Character-building starts when we begin to acquire the right attitude (the way we view something), and the right attitude starts when we know and understand more. Knowing and understanding comes when we search in the right places, and God, through the Holy Spirit, opens our "eyes" (understanding) to things we'd never seen before.

For me to gain the correct attitude towards this step, there were a few things I needed to understand. I will explain these things in the way I believe the Holy Spirit revealed them to me, working through the Program and also with my mentor. Again, at the time I worked through this step I had no understanding of anything. I just did what I was told with honesty and willingness because I really wanted it. I have put down my understanding of how it all worked for me because I think it might bring a bit of clarity to you, but if you don't understand what I'm on about, it won't matter, just as long as you do the work honestly and willingly.

The first thing I needed to grasp was what exactly it was that I wanted God to do for me. Quite simply, I wanted Him to change me. I was getting ready to *repent,* with the firm belief and understanding that only He could help me do this with any real conviction. Under the word "repent" in the Oxford dictionary, we find the following meaning: "Resolve not to continue wrongdoing in, (action . . .)." What strikes me about this definition is that we are making a *decision,* a resolve, to turn away from our wrong action. Having got this far in the book you will know that of ourselves we do not have the power to do so, while maintaining the right motive as well. For instance, if someone said they'd give me a large sum of money to be nice to someone who is being horrible and whom I don't like for, say, an hour, I could easily be as sweet as pie to them for that period of time. I would grin and bear it for the hour, because my motive was the thought of a wad of notes in my pocket at the end. The problem is that with the wrong motive I could only be nice for a short time, no matter how much I was offered thereafter, because my true feelings and attitude towards that person would come out. Only God can give us the right attitude and enough power to change our defects of character, and this only if certain conditions are met.

The first condition is willingness, we've got to *want* to change. I love the scene from the movie *The Breakup* when Jennifer Aniston says to Vince Vaughn that he doesn't help her with the dishes.

He retorts that if she wants him to do them, she must just ask.

She then says that she doesn't want him to just do them, she wants him to *want* to do them.

He replies, "Who *wants* to do dishes?"

What she really means is that he should have the right attitude towards doing the dishes. It should be a case of him taking pleasure in easing her load and wanting to do something that shows he loves and cares for her.

I think God sees it in much the same light. For me, the bulk of this step was becoming willing to have these defects removed.

A Christian who battles with gossip will go to the extreme of exposing another's extramarital affair by praying aloud for that person to see the error of their ways. If you ask the person who prayed whether they like a gossip, they'll give you a straight, "No, not at all!" You might wonder why they do it then . . . Well, this person will probably say that praying for another is not gossip, but rather concerned love and care. I do not believe this to be true, because if they really cared, they would not hurt that person by publicizing their affair. People gossip either because it makes them feel superior to others or because they want the attention as others listen, and this gives them a sense of self-worth or importance. Both reasons are self-centred. However, people generally know that nobody likes a gossip, so they disguise it as spiritual charity. They often start off by saying something like, "I hate to gossip, but as a Christian, watching my Christian sister going down the wrong path . . ." They then proceed to rip the other person to shreds.

The point is that if you would ask this person whether they wanted God to remove this defect of gossip from their lives, they'd either say they are not a gossip, or they would still want to be able to talk about people "in a loving and helpful way". A person with this defect would not want to let go of being able to talk about others because when people listen to them, it eases the pain of rejection and being ignored. Do you see how this pans out? The real defect of character is a feeling of rejection. The rejection can be real or imagined but is normally only a perception on their part, it is most often not reality.

I speak here from my own experiences in my life, as I suffered with rejection and enjoyed telling stories that everyone wanted to hear.

There are other defects that are downplayed, such as when we say, "Hate is not murder," or, "Lust is not rape," or, "Comfort food is not gluttony," or, "Ambition is not greed," and so on. However, any of these can become the extreme given the right circumstances. If we are living with defects, even at low levels, and are saying that they are part of us and we are just trying to live with them, we will be miserable, and they will just get worse over time.[39]

The reason we do not want to let go and let God undertake with both the gossip and the rejection, for example, is that we do not really trust that He will remove these defects. We are also not entirely convinced that He is capable of being the comfort we were receiving from the attention invoked by the gossip if He does get rid of the gossip and rejection. Does this mean we're done for? Absolutely not. This is where the Program champions over anything else I have ever come across. I never had to understand any of this back then, I just needed *honesty, willingness* and *patience.* Nothing more was required. Desperation had brought me to the Program, the Program told me what to do, and this allowed God to work. Simply tell God that you do not have enough strength to believe that He can remove these defects, that you really want them to be removed because you see them as wrong, but that you feel afraid of being alone and having no one who cares about you and sees you as worthy. Ask God to give you the strength and willingness you will need, and then move on. You do not need to worry about whether it has worked or not. The goal in this Program is the *journey,* not the destination. While we are on the journey we are forging a relationship with God, and this relationship will give us the ability to live peacefully, joyfully and comfortably with ourselves. When we are in this state we are the most useful to God through His plans for us. I believe the destiny will be reached in the next life – in eternity.

The next thing is that we must be willing to forgive. We

39. See Matthew 5:22, 27-28.

must be willing to forgive others, ourselves and even God. Notice that I said we must become *willing* to forgive, we do not necessarily have to forgive straight away. Forgiveness can be very difficult for many people, as some hurts run deep. I put it to you, though, that none of the hurts inflicted on us run deeper than the ones we've inflicted on God.

You might have noticed that I mentioned we need to become willing to forgive God as well. This was no mistake, but I will need to explain it because as we know, God is perfect.

We do not and will not fully understand all of God's ways of doing things and will not always think they're fair.

For my thoughts are not your thoughts, neither are your ways my ways, saith the LORD. Isaiah 55:8

Yet ye say, The way of the LORD is not equal. Hear now, O house of Israel; Is not my way equal? are not your ways unequal? Ezekiel 18:25

Consequently, we will be hurt by certain things that come from God which we will perceive as wrong, but which are not, because He is God and His ways are perfect.[40] Nevertheless, because there are some things we will never fully understand in this lifetime, we can hold onto hurts or resentments towards God which we can only let go of through forgiveness. I do not believe this is being blasphemous because we are truly trying to right our relationship with God as best we know how, and I believe He understands this.

---

40. See Deuteronomy 32:4.

We might wonder why we need to be willing to forgive. The reason is quite simple really. By asking God to remove our defects of character, we are also asking Him to forgive us of our wrongs. In order for Him to forgive us, though, we must first forgive others. I do not fully understand this, but the Bible is clear on this matter:

But if ye do not forgive, neither will your Father which is in heaven forgive your trespasses. Mark 11:26

God knows if we're not strong enough to forgive everyone everything, but as long as we are honestly willing, He will provide the strength needed at the right time. Even if we do not have the willingness to forgive, but we are prepared to be honest about that fact, He will work in that area of our lives at the appropriate time.

Here is a summary of the action I had to take. I had to *want* to have my defects removed. Having completed Step 4, I knew that my basic character defects were (or stemmed from) that I was selfish, self-seeking, dishonest, inconsiderate and afraid. When I found that I did not have the willingness for certain character flaws on my list to be changed, I needed to ask God to give me that willingness. There was nothing more I could do but to continue to ask for that willingness until it came. But I did not just sit and wait for the willingness to come concerning those few character flaws that I did not sincerely want removed; what I did was I got on with the rest of the steps. Over time the willingness did come.

Once more, remember that establishing a meaningful relationship with God is the journey and not a specific goal.

As long as we are on the journey, we will be exactly where we are supposed to be, regardless of whether we have just started or have been at it for a long while. I love this!

The action for Step 6

1) Review your defects of character from Step 4 and 5. Do you fully agree that you are generally selfish, self-seeking, dishonest, inconsiderate and/or afraid?

   If your answer is "no" to having any of these defects of character, I suggest you pray and ask God to reveal them to you. Here is a prayer you can pray out aloud on your own:

   "Dear Lord and heavenly Father, I am once again faced with a dilemma over which I am totally powerless. I hear what is being said, but I do not believe that I am selfish, self-seeking, dishonest, inconsiderate or afraid. Lord, if this is the path to a close and intimate relationship with You, please open my eyes to see these defects, if I have them. I want to be totally open with You and I want to proceed without pretending I believe what is suggested I should believe. I ask that You reveal my defects to me, in Jesus' name. Amen."

   I recommend you do not continue further until you can agree you have all or some of these defects. Once you receive this revelation (I believe you will if you are sincere), you can continue.

2) Are you willing and ready for God to remove these character defects?

If you feel you are not ready to have them removed for whatever reason, you need to pray for that willingness. Here is a prayer you can pray:

"Dear Father God, I realize that I have certain defects of character that are ultimately blocking me off from the truly intimate relationship You want with me, and which I sincerely desire to have with You. For reasons known [name them] or unknown to me, I am not willing to accept that they be removed. However, I believe this could be the way to relieving the blockages that block me off from a deeper relationship with You, and I ask that You give me a real desire to have them removed by You. In Jesus' name. Amen."

3) Once you are able to answer "yes" to the two questions above, you are ready for Step 7.

Step 7

We humbly asked God to remove our shortcomings.

(Humility)

Humble yourselves in the sight of the Lord, and He shall lift you up. James 4:10

"I can't, but through me, God can."

Once we can truly believe this statement, doing Step 7 is easy. I have discussed a bit about my understanding of humility in Chapter 4. I would, however, like to reiterate some points because it's one of the most vital elements to attaining God's strength and power in our lives.

Why, as human beings, are we so prone to be restless, irritable and discontented – in a word, miserable? I believe it's because we don't understand God's will for us and don't trust that He will truly meet our needs. We are uncomfortable and worried about losing what we have and also about not getting what we want. Because of this, we try to control the management of our lives. We may acknowledge that God is our creator, but we want to tell Him what to do with us.

But now, O LORD, thou art our father; we are the clay,
and thou our potter; and we all are the work of thy hand.

Isaiah 64:8

It would be ridiculous if a lump of clay being moulded into a plate suddenly piped up to the potter, "Hey, hang on a minute, pal . . . I'm not going to be a plate, I'm going to be a vase, so you had better shape me as such!" We would laugh at this concept, and yet this is in effect what we do to God all the time.

The cause of this response from us is a lack of trust in Him, and a focus on our own expectations and ambitions. As long as we do not trust God with our lives, we will try to run them ourselves, or we will try dictating to God what we want Him to do for us. We come to Him in prayer to meet the needs that will fulfil our plans when really, we ought to come to Him each day expecting direction, guidance and to be equipped for whichever direction He wishes to lead us in. We need to *trust* that where we are and what we are doing at this precise moment in time is exactly where He wants us to be and what He wants us to be doing, even if it doesn't feel nice.

You turn things upside down [with your perversity]!
Shall the potter be considered equal with the clay, That
the thing that is made would say to its maker, "He did
not make me"; Or the thing that is formed say to him
who formed it, "He has no understanding"?

Isaiah 29:16 (AMP)

I cannot run my own life; my creator *has* to. He designed me and I will function best according to the specifications

He has laid down for me. He does not hand me the entire manual for each day specifically, but He issues a general manual (the Bible) for the workings of the human being. Just as a small child does not know what it will do each day, so we too will not know the exact plan of what we will be doing each day. The child has been given certain instructions to follow each day: get up at 7am, wash your face and brush your teeth, get dressed, come down and eat your breakfast, etc. For the rest, the child waits expectantly to see what their parent(s) will come up with each day. I believe this is exactly what our heavenly Father wants us to do. God may give us vision and a heart for the path He is leading us in, but we do not know when, where, how, for how long, and with whom this path will happen. This is perhaps why Jesus said:

And said, Verily I say unto you, Except ye be converted, and become as little children, ye shall not enter into the kingdom of heaven. Matthew 18:3

It is vital that we don't know the implementation method of His purpose for our lives because if we did, we would have a field day trying to orchestrate just how it would need to be done – our egos are just that big. I realized that as long as I thought I had an actual role to play in the running of my life, I could not surrender to God. The irony is that the only role I have to play in my life *is* the surrender of my will to Him, and this is actually the only thing God has ever given me control over in life. All other control and effect I thought I had was just an illusion. The pursuit of this illusion is what created my defects of character in the first place. God is the creator; He is in control and He has the power to change my life totally. When I can grasp this,

I am able to attain a semblance of humility. What God does not have control over is my *will*; as I said previously, He actually made it that way. With humility in place, I am able to hand my will back to Him, and then I am ready to ask Him to remove my shortcomings.

Motive is very important for this step. We need to once again consider why we want these shortcomings removed. An obvious reason can be the realization of the immense pain these shortcomings are causing *you;* this was certainly true for me in the beginning. However, our shortcomings also cause pain to others and to God. Pain is a great teacher, but at this stage of the Program it is possible to get one's mind focused on a purer motive. I do not feel it is imperative to be able to reach this so-called purer motive in order to achieve humility, but as we need to continue growing to survive, it will help a lot to see in which direction we need to go. Ultimately, we need to start living a life that is focused on the salvation and well-being of others.

With this in mind I was able to see that in order for me to even begin to think of others and be of assistance to them, I was going to have to be rid of my shortcomings – my character defects. Being selfish, dishonest, self-seeking, frightened and inconsiderate all point me in the opposite direction to the way God has designed my life to work. If I am to be of any help whatsoever to my fellow man, I *must* be rid of these defects. This understanding really was an immense help to me in having the right attitude (one of humility) towards asking God to remove my shortcomings.

The action for Step 7

To complete Step 7, all it takes is two prayers.

At the stage, get your Step 4 Fears inventory worksheets out in front of you. For the first prayer it will help to refer to the list of fears on your worksheets, and bear these fears in mind as you pray. These are not our only shortcomings, but they do form part of them:

1) For the first prayer, I recommend the following:

   "Dear heavenly Father, I am now willing that You should have all of me, good and bad. I pray that You now remove from me every single defect of character which stands in the way of my usefulness to You and those around me. Grant me strength, as I go from here, to do Your bidding. I ask this all in Jesus' name. Amen."

2) The second prayer can be:

   "Dear heavenly Father, I realize that without You I am nothing. I ask that You continue to keep my motives pure and that You alert me to any change in attitude along my recovery journey. I ask this in Jesus' name. Amen."

You are now ready to continue to Step 8.

Step 8

We made a list of all persons we
had harmed, and became willing
to make amends to them all.

(Preparation)

Therefore, if thou bring thy gift to the altar, and there
rememberest that thy brother hath ought against
thee; Leave there thy gift before the altar, and go thy
way; first be reconciled to thy brother, and then come
and offer thy gift.   Matthew 5:23-24

I find that Steps 2, 6 and 8 are very similar in that they
all require a process, which can take time. I'm not saying
that they cannot be achieved in an instant, but they
most definitely require God's help. In Step 2 we "*came* to
believe", in Step 6 we were "*entirely* ready", and in Step 8
we "*became* willing". All these phrases seem to suggest a
process of acquiring a certain attitude, which stems from
a new understanding. The reason I say that they will require
God's help is that if we could attain this way of thinking
on our own, we would have had that new understanding
already. Most of us realized some things were not right

inside us and maybe even what was causing these things, but we lacked the power to change anything. I am so grateful that God was there with the power needed to get me through these steps, I just had to be willing and ready for Him to work. However, because of the fact that human nature (self, ego and pride) prevents God from working, a process is required to break it down (humility), and this can take time.

What is meant by *make amends*? It sounds simple enough, but is it? I have heard many people refer to Step 8 and 9 as "cleaning their side of the street". The step does require that, but it is not quite as simple as that.

Just "cleaning my side of the street" would avoid a lot of embarrassment and would allow me to keep my assumed dignity intact. I say *assumed dignity*, because although this is how I perceived it, it was in fact my *pride* I was keeping intact, and it is this very pride that unknowingly prevents me from accepting God's gift of grace, which in this instance is His power and ability to overcome. What God really wants in making amends is *restitution*. The definition of this word describes exactly what our goal in making amends should be: "A return to or restoration of a previous state or position".[41]

What we are trying to do with the people we have harmed is to restore our relationship with them to its previous state – or better if possible. I am not naïve enough to think this possible with everyone, but it should be our goal and motive. God can do many things, but He cannot choose for

---

41. The American Heritage® Stedman's Medical Dictionary (copyright © 2002, 2001, 1995 by Houghton Mifflin Company).

a person. He gave us free will and this gift stops Him from being able to decide for us. There are going to be people who might politely accept our apologies but may still want nothing to do with us. We do not try to force them, or even blame them. Through our own defective[42] interactions with them, we may have hurt some people deeply, and it will require the grace of God in their lives to free them from the bondage of unforgiveness. We need to accept this and walk away. I think this is what was really meant by "cleaning our side of the street", but it shouldn't end there. We need to pray for them, pray that God's love and grace will be made available to them as it was for us. However, we should not feel guilty about what we have done in the past. We are not doormats to be walked on and should not grovel or beg for forgiveness. As long as we are sincere in making our amends, we know that the Lord sees our hearts and He can restore us.

Part of making our amends involves asking God for His forgiveness. In fact, this is most important. It is a wonderful thing to know that He *always* forgives us:

If we confess our sins, he is faithful and just to forgive us our sins, and to cleanse us from all unrighteousness.

1 John 1:9

---

42. We are talking about our defects of character: selfish, self-centred, dishonest, frightened or inconsiderate. It may be that at the time of our interactions with someone, we were unaware of situations or circumstances the other person may have, things like a bereavement or mental health. Our response may seem appropriate, but due to the fact that we never considered these options in their lives, our response may have hurt them. It is important to remember that even though it was done through ignorant inconsideration, it is still a harm that we need to take responsibility for and make amends. Here, it is all about cleaning our side of the street and restoring our relationship with God, and then trusting that He may affect a restoration of relationship with the other person in due course.

I have often found that many of the people who did not want to restore our relationship came back to me later on and restitution was possible. I truly believe that prayer helped in these situations. Sadly, though, some relationships are never restored, yet I believe that continually praying for these people might help them eventually restore or develop a relationship with God, and this is far more important a relationship than the one we might have with them. In all the amends I was able to make, only one person outright wanted nothing to do with me, and I continued praying for that person as God's grace allowed me to, and my hope is that they, too, will find serenity in a true relationship with God. I would say about 80 per cent of the amends I made to date have ended up in restitution, and this has given me immense peace in my heart.

The question as to why we need to restore relationships is a key element of our existence, and I feel it will help to share my views on it. The Bible states:

Now ye are the body of Christ, and members in particular.

1 Corinthians 12:27

Everybody on this earth is God's creation, and therefore a potential member of Christ's body.[43] If we take a normal body with its various parts (members) – arms, legs, kidneys, skin, etc. – there is *constant* communication going on in order for that body to function and operate optimally. We can even go as far as to say that each part of the body is working and functioning in *relation* to the others, and they have to in order to continue proper communication. If there is a breakdown in communication

---

43. See 2 Corinthians 6:18 and Galatians 3:26.

within a body, it malfunctions and does not operate at its optimal design proficiency. The same applies to the body of Christ. There is, however, one major difference and this is where the comparison breaks down. God has chosen us – those members of his body who are in communication with him – to work to restore relationships with the parts that are missing or malfunctioning. He wants us to help the other person to "sweep their side of the street", where permitted. Not necessarily by doing it for them, but by the example of change they see in us and by passing on the message of how that happened in our lives.

This is why relationships are so important to God because He wants the body of Christ to be fully functional. In restoring relationships, we reopen the channels of communication, and God (through the Holy Spirit) is able to speak into the lives of others once more, using *us* as channels. I cannot say for sure why God chose this way to do things, but I believe it could be a way for a person who does not know God to be able to hear His message through another bodily being. It also gives us an opportunity to form a relationship of love and support with another person. More than this, though, I believe that it is so that He can develop a deeper, more meaningful relationship with us personally. My wife and I planned our wedding together; I supplied the funds, and she chose what she wanted (just kidding). We spent a lot of time and many long discussions organizing everything, and in doing it this way we grew to know each other. I delighted her with one or two extra surprises, and I think God woos us along the way with surprises of His own.

This is part of what loving is all about, and God is love and He wants as many ways as possible to express His love, which is why He created us. If we are to be in relationship with Him and part of His kingdom, we need to learn to love and this includes loving what God loves, which is His creation. So, we start first with the people we know, and that is why we need to strive to make restitution with them during our amends. This is the attitude God is going to place in our hearts. Right now, if we start to grasp this concept and push through with the amends in the next step, God will embed the right attitude in our hearts without us even realizing it.

When you work through this step at the end of this chapter, you will see that I suggest going back to the Step 4 (Harms and Resentments) worksheets to write down all harms and all resentments for where you recognize you played a part in another's harm towards you.

We often forget two important points as far as others' hurts towards us go. One is that they too are battling with their own character defects. We often fail to realize that we do not have the monopoly on character defects, most people suffer from them as well.[44] The second point is that, rightly or wrongly, the other person may feel we had been hurting them for a long time before they finally reacted, and quite often we had been hurting them without realizing it. So many of the resentments we have built up because of what others have done to us are actually due to their reaction to something they felt we did to them first. We may feel that a person driving a bulldozer through our boundary wall a

---

44. This is why I strongly believe that anyone who is really battling with a specific character defect in their lives will be able to overcome it by simply working the same steps – you just replace the word "ourselves" in Step 1, with the defect of character you are battling with, and then work it through the steps in the same manner. You should try to keep that defect of character in the forefront of your mind as you go through the steps again.

bit harsh after we only bumped the corner of theirs the day before, but we are not to focus on their wrongs at all. The fact of the matter is that we *did* in fact harm them and we want to make restitution for that. Before we are able to go to them and ask for forgiveness for our part, we need to forgive them for theirs, even if they do not ask for it.[45]

We are trying to restore and build a relationship with God, and ultimately it will be His forgiveness that is important. Others are required to forgive us in the same manner, but if they do not, God is able to forgive us and remove anything that might bind us. We let that remain between them and God, but we still pray for that restitution between them and Him, and we release them through our forgiveness.

Now that we have our list of amends in place and have been able to adopt the right attitude towards the people we have resented and then hurt, we should now be willing to make our amends.

The action for Step 8

Download the Amends worksheet[46] or draw up a blank template on a piece of paper from my example on page 223. You will see my example of how to choose your "Name of the party harmed". This was taken from my Resentments and Harms worksheets.

---

45. It is important not to go to someone and say, "I forgive you", unless they have specifically acknowledged harming or hurting you in some way, because they may build resentment towards us because of what they could construe as arrogance. We forgive them in our hearts and declare it to the Lord.
46. https://www.malcolmdown.co.uk/worksheets

1) Go back to your Resentments Inventory worksheet from Step 4 and check column 5 ("Future action") for any resentments that have "and make amends" written down. On your Amends worksheets, under the first column ("Name of the party harmed"), write down all the people/institutions from your Resentments worksheet that were marked "and make amends" in the fifth column.

2) Take out your Harms Inventory worksheet from Step 4 as well, and here on the Amends worksheet, under the first column ("Name of the party harmed"), copy all the people/institutions from the first column ("The harm"). You will not need to duplicate the ones taken off your Resentment Inventory worksheets.

3) If there is any other harm that you might have subsequently inflicted, or some that come to mind that are not on your Step 4 worksheet, write them in as well.

4) I suggest praying the following prayer, so that you can be sure that you are not missing any:

"Dear heavenly Father, I want to thank You for bringing me this far. I realize the importance of making my amends with all the people whom I have harmed, and do not want to miss any. I ask You to please reveal to me any persons/institutions I might have overlooked so that I can include them in my lists. Thank You for helping me. In Jesus' name. Amen."

Now that you have completed Step 8, keep your Amends worksheet with you as you proceed to Step 9.

Personal Example of My Amends Worksheet

	Name of the party harmed	Prayer and meditation	Immediate amends (I) or deferred amends (D – put approximate time and date)	No direct contact	Check when done
1.	My mum				
2.	Girl from Surrey				
3.	Old school				
4.	Bricklayer				

The first 2 names in the first column were taken from my example Step 4 Resentments worksheet and the second 2 from my Harms worksheet

Step 9

We made direct amends to such people whenever possible, except when to do so would injure them or others.

(Action)

Give, and it shall be given unto you; good measure, pressed down, and shaken together, and running over, shall men give into your bosom. For with the same measure that ye mete withal it shall be measured to you again.   Luke 6:38

Here is a powerful but uncomfortable step. I say uncomfortable because it requires being humbled, and, as mentioned previously, the humbling process is not fun. However, it was after this step that I started to experience the true power of God at work in my life. It was during this step that I became aware of the fact that I was not alone, that *something* was doing for me what I could never do for myself. What an immense sense of freedom and peace that gave me! For the first time since beginning the Program, I realized that my life was not being run by me. I knew after this that I did not *need* to try and orchestrate or control my life. When I started this step, I had to stick my pride in my pocket and get to it, and I am pleased that the Lord was there to help me with this part.

Continuing on from the previous step; now that we have the right attitude and motive for making our amends we then need to use the most effective means and acquire sufficient courage to make the best amends possible. I was once told by an old pastor of mine, "Rory, you can be right, but wrong at the top of your voice." How we do these amends is important. It cannot be achieved by ourselves or by the help of another human being, we *must* go to God – I love this fact. I find His power always comes through for me in the end if I remain in His will. I know that I am in His will if I have given everything over to Him and have asked Him to take control. From then on in, the process has started. We are where we are, and that is exactly where God wants us to be.

This means that God will orchestrate our amends exactly as they are meant to take place. So, we can really relax and do our best in each case, knowing that the outcome will be in God's hands, and after making our amends we can leave guilt-free, no matter what the outcome is. Just as God cannot choose for us, He cannot choose the other person's reaction. All He can do is reveal the truth to them. If there is not a full restitution of relationship after a particular amend has been made, we can walk away knowing that our relationship with God is strengthened. I feel, though, that we should still pray for the other person that they may find peace and joy in a relationship with God themselves. Very often, over time the relationship between the other person and ourselves is restored as God heals their heart.

Through my own experience I have found that I cannot really give any hard and fast rules about how to make each amends; all I can give you is a brief overview. As I said before, attitude and motivation are important, but we also need to be true to our heart. What I mean by this is that when deciding on whether to make direct contact or not, for instance, we need to search our hearts as to why we want to make whichever amend in a certain way.

Let's look at a hypothetical example. A man working through this step might decide to tell his wife of an extramarital affair he was having many years ago, but upon reflection he realizes that the only reason he wants to tell her is to be rid of the guilt he is feeling. In this instance, he needs to carefully consider whether he should make that revelation or not. If his motive, now that he has stopped it and is serving the Lord, is to continue his relationship with his wife in total honesty and does not want his wife to be embarrassed in public if it is ever revealed, this might be a better motive. However, he needs to truly look at the bigger picture: are there children involved, is she strong enough to handle a revelation of this magnitude, is she the type of person who wants to know this sort of information? He also needs to bear in mind who else might be affected by the revelation. It may be better for him to say something like this:

"In the past, I have done some wrong things for which I am not proud. I have been dishonest, selfish and inconsiderate . . . and I know I have hurt you. I ask your forgiveness and want you to know that I am truly sorry for my behaviour. I have handed my life over to God and am following a Program which I believe is bringing me into a much deeper relationship with God. I love you and want to restore our relationship so that I can be someone who will support you, and on whom you can rely."

Having said this, I believe that if she were to ask him outright if he has had an affair, he should tell her the truth.

Unfortunately, there is very little other advice I can give on how to make your amends. That is why I keep stressing the need to go to God. He knows everything there is to know about the various scenarios and if you hand it over to Him, what needs to be done will come to you. If you feel there is no prompting, maybe leave it a week or so and continue praying. After this, I suggest you follow your gut-instinct, because a lot of the time this is the way the Holy Spirit prompts us.

Sometimes during an amends, you might find that the person needs to let off a little steam. Once again there is no hard and fast rule on whether you need to sit and "weather the storm", or if you should "beetle off" out the door. Personally, I would sit and allow them a little time to vent. If they start getting too heavy or aggressive, I would then politely excuse myself and leave. Whatever you choose to do, one suggestion stands: do not argue back and do not bring up their wrongs or harms. I find this easier when I remind myself that they too may be ill and cannot always react in a sensible way. I also remind myself that the harms I caused them could have been quite severe.

The order in which to make amends is another debate that has no real right or wrong answers. When I made my amends I started with the ones that were easiest and closest to where I lived. I left the difficult ones for later, and the ones I felt were impossible, I did not think about at that stage. I found that as I made the easier amends with little or no ill feeling from the other person, it became easier to do the more difficult ones. By the time I had got through the bulk of them, the ones I had thought were impossible now seemed quite doable. Many say this is an obvious progression as a person's self-confidence grows. This could be partly true, but I believe more in God's divine intervention. I think that as we take the first step "into the waters of the Jordan river",[47] so to speak, the waters then part and we can walk across the river on dry ground. There is very little we can do but to *start* making the amends. We start with the things that we can do, and as we do so I believe the power of the Holy Spirit fills us with the strength to get through the others. I always try to keep my primary motive in the forefront of my mind when making difficult amends. I am trying to clear the way so that I can have a deeper relationship with God. It actually has very little to do with the person or institution with whom I am making the amends; it really has more to do with the Lord and myself.

The action for Step 9

1) Have your Amends worksheet from Step 8 next to you and carefully go through my example on pages 233 to 234. My example and explanations should help you with how you go about doing yours.

2) Column 2 can be actioned right away. Go back to the relevant worksheets from Step 4 (Resentments

---

47. See Joshua 3:13-16.

and Harms) and see what the nature of your various harms were. In your prayer, ask for God's forgiveness, for His blessing on the corresponding person or institution, and for His hand to be on the amends process. Here is a prayer you can use:

"Dear heavenly Father, in my past dealings with [name each person from your amends list in here as you pray for each one individually], I realize I was [list all the defects you marked in column 4 ("My part") of your Step 4 Resentments worksheet] and I possibly hurt them, which might have caused them to retaliate. I ask Your forgiveness for hurting You as well as them, and I ask that You bless and protect them. I ask that You relieve them of any bondage I might have caused them, that they might prosper. I ask for You to be in control of this mending process for all parties involved, and I ask that as many relationships be restored as possible. I ask all this in Jesus' name. Amen."

When you are praying this prayer, keep this person in your thoughts. You can do a prayer and amend to God for each person in succession or do each on the day of each amends; it's up to you.

3) After praying, take a minute or two to be quiet; God will disclose to you in His own way and time what He wants you to know and understand. Often He gives you the peace and strength you need to continue through the process of amends during this time. If nothing seems to come, do not be disheartened; you have what you need, and it will become apparent in its time. You can now confidently tick the "Prayer and meditation" box next to this name.

4) Now start column 3 – immediate amends (I) or deferred amends (D). I suggest you pray again and ask God for His wisdom and guidance:

"Dear heavenly Father, I know that You are omniscient (all-knowing) and omnipotent (all-powerful), so I come to You to ask You for wisdom, discretion, sincerity and courage when making amends to [give the person's/institution's name]. I thank You for Your help and guidance. In Jesus' name. Amen."

5) If you have indicated an immediate amends, pick up the phone and arrange a time with the person as soon as possible. Each person and situation might be different, so I suggest organizing and doing the amends with each one as soon as you can, in your own way, without procrastinating.

Note: You must make sure you do not bring up or refer to the harm the other person might have done. This makes the apology seem insincere and as a result of what they did. It is also important to know that in order for us to restore our relationship with them and God, we cannot be taking stock of their wrongs and harms.

Here is an example template of what I used to say:

"_____ [put the name of the person off the amends list here], in my previous dealings with you and/or your company, I was selfish, dishonest, frightened and inconsiderate, and I realize that I hurt you and caused your company a loss of _____ [if that is the case]. I apologize for doing this and would like to pay you back the money in two instalments of

_____ each, starting with the first payment on the 30th of this month. [You will obviously make an offer to pay any money back as soon as possible, making sure that your family needs are met, and making sure you do not go into debt. If it is a large sum of money, you may just suggest to the person that you work out a repayment scheme together that would be amenable to both parties.] I trust this will be acceptable, and I wish you and your company all the best in future."

6) Tick off each amends as you do them in the "Check when done" column.

7) If you have an amend to make for which you cannot make direct contact, tick column 4 "No direct contact",[48] and then tick column 5 ("Check when done") after you have done your prayer and meditation for this person in column 2 ("Prayer and meditation").

8) If you feel that you would like to write a letter or send a message, then keep it short, using the same example as for a direct amends. However, you must be honest with yourself and make sure that it is not fear that is keeping you from making a face-to-face amends.

You can proceed to Step 10 as soon as you have been through your Amends worksheet thoroughly, making sure that you have a definite plan for each amends not yet completed – this should include times and dates for the outstanding amends.

---

48. This could include situations where you could cause harm by making a direct amends, like someone you had an affair with. It could also be that the person is deceased, or it could be that you have tried and failed to locate them.

How I filled in the Amends worksheet

Column

Prayer and Meditation	I tick all the harms, under the "Prayer and meditation" column, because we should always pray and think before we do anything. My main harm was always to the Lord, and I want to restore my relationship with Him. After praying, I spend a bit of time thinking over the harm, and just leave time for God to speak to me. He normally does this through thoughts, and I gain clarity of understanding.
Immediate amends (I) or deferred amends (D)	*My mum* – it is an immediate and direct amends because she is close by, and I want to make restitution (restore our relationship).

Girl from Surrey – I am married, and she might be too. I do not want to make any direct contact with her, as this could cause complications in both our relationships. I therefore put N/A (not applicable).

Old school – my old school is in another province and the teachers there are not the ones who were there when I was there, so I will write a letter. I will do it in November this year when my work is winding down.

Bricklayer – I will see him at work tomorrow and will make an appointment with him at 4pm when the workers are packing up, and make my amends.

Personal Example of My Amends Worksheet

	Name of the party harmed	Prayer and meditation	Immediate amends (I) or deferred amends (D – put approximate time and date)	No direct contact	Check when done
1.	My mum	✓	I – immediate		✓
2.	Girl from Surrey	✓	N/A	✓	✓
3.	Old school	✓	D – December this year		
4.	Bricklayer	✓	D – Tomorrow, 4pm		

Step 10

We continued to take personal inventory, and when we were wrong, promptly admitted it.

(Maintenance)

For I say, through the grace given unto me, to every man that is among you, not to think of himself more highly than he ought to think; but to think soberly, according as God hath dealt to every man the measure of faith. Romans 12:3

Step 10, in a nutshell, is a combination of Steps 4, 8 and 9. You will not redo all your resentments, fears and harms that you have already done, but rather for the day or even moment that new ones come up. Steps 10, 11 and 12 are going to be your new design for living. They will form the basis for the rest of your journey into eternity, and you will use them every day. In order for us to maintain a spiritual relationship with our Father God, we need to keep our spiritual channels unblocked. Step 10 is essentially a structured practical system of achieving this. If our lives were a car, Step 10 is the servicing of that car.

If you have reached this point in the Program, you will almost certainly have had a spiritual awakening. This could feel like everything to you or nothing much at all, but it can be recognized by the fact that there will be a peace and awareness of *something* that was not there before. If you are still feeling miserable, I would say that there is possibly something you are holding back on, and my suggestion would be to work through the steps from 1 to 9 again (remember the teaching on perseverance from page 82). I have heard many stories, each one different from mine, from people who received the power to overcome many of their defects, power which they never had before. We all have "thorns in the flesh" and "crosses to bear" that might have been placed there for a reason, otherwise our egos would take our lives back from God's hands again.

Paul said:

> *And lest I should be exalted above measure through the abundance of the revelations, there was given to me a thorn in the flesh, the messenger of Satan to buffet me, lest I should be exalted above measure.*
>
> 2 Corinthians 12:7

And Jesus said:

> *If any man will come after me, let him deny himself, and take up his cross daily, and follow me.*   Luke 9:23

I spent a lot of time pondering the words of these two verses, as most of what I'd heard of God were nice, comfortable things. A "thorn in the flesh" and "a cross to bear" both sounded like pain and discomfort to me, and yet both are mentioned as part of being a follower of Christ. What I came to realize was that God wants me in a relationship with Him *all* the time. The problem is that I don't listen too well. In his book *The Problem of Pain*,[49] C.S. Lewis notes:

We can ignore even pleasure. But pain insists upon being attended to. God whispers to us in our pleasures, speaks in our conscience, but shouts in our pains: it is his megaphone to rouse a deaf world.

Thankfully, God never leaves us without comfort. Jesus said:

Come unto me, all ye that labour and are heavy laden, and I will give you rest. Take my yoke upon you, and learn of me; for I am meek and lowly in heart: and ye shall find rest unto your souls. For my yoke is easy, and my burden is light. Matthew 11:28-30

This speaks of coming with pain and burden and finding rest, of taking up Jesus' mission *with* Him, learning of Him and finding rest in our souls, and finally that promise that *His* mission and burden are easy and light. Is this not what we are all looking for: rest for our bodies, rest for our souls, and a mission and burden that are easy and light? They can be, if our "yoke" is God's. His yoke (meaning mission, love, passion) is His people, His lost creations.

These days nothing gives me more pain than not being in right relationship with God, and nothing keeps me out of relationship with Him more than not being in right relationship with my fellow man. This is why this step is so vital. I have to do my inventories continually so that I can right my wrongs with others and gain motivation

---

49. *The Problem of Pain* by C.S. Lewis © copyright 1940 C.S. Lewis Pte Ltd.

through seeing my positive growth. This ultimately leads to a continuous unhindered relationship with my heavenly Father. It is an incredible journey. I am sure that as you practise using this step in your life daily, it will become habitual, as I found it came to me after a while.

Once a year I spend some time reflecting on the main events of the past twelve months of my life. It gives me a general overview of my progress and if anything stands out as *pain,* I review who or what caused it, what it did to me inside, and how I reacted to it. I look at my part and am able to go and make my amends. It may seem unnecessary, given that we take a daily inventory, however I find that I have often overlooked small offences or resentment which has built up over time. This process also allows me to see how my life has progressed with God's help over that year, and this gives me renewed hope and strength.

Consider a soldier fighting in a World War I trench in France. He has fought for a year in the mud and cold, winning a piece of ground today, losing a piece tomorrow. By the time a year is up, he must feel like he hasn't done much at all, and that it was all an absolute waste of time. What if once a year he was taken off the battlefront and shown a map of France? What if he could see on the map that over the last year they had conquered more than a third of the enemy-held country? I am pretty sure this would give the boy renewed hope and energy. Because I have been engaged in spiritual warfare on different fronts during the year, I have often been unable to view the bigger picture. I feel like that soldier must have felt; like I'm swimming in treacle and not going anywhere. I find that an annual inventory is like getting out of the trenches and looking at the map of my advancement. I get renewed hope and excitement at what God is doing in my life.

A daily inventory is more about that particular day's activities and is usually quite easy. When you start to work Step 10 at the end of this chapter you will find that I have made up a shortened worksheet which combine Steps 4, 8 and 9. It is easy to use, puts things into perspective very quickly, and shouldn't take more than a few minutes to do. During the course of the day, I might have a worker, let's call him Fabio, who mixes building sand for screeding a concrete floor instead of using the correct sharp sand. I have shown him the difference and shown him which pile is which. The lad is from Mozambique and answers yes to anything I ask him, and I know this. He has wasted four cubic meters of sand and nine bags of cement, which is at a cost to the business. Instead of explaining to him that this is wrong and that he may have to pay some of the money back through extra work, I get angry and give him a mouthful. I tell him what I think of him and that he shouldn't be working here. After this encounter, even though I am feeling the pain inside me because of this outburst, I do not have the peace and calm to recognize my mistake and to make amends. (This is what I am striving towards, though, and eventually, with God's power, I will not do this at all.) I carry this pain with me the whole day and it puts a bit of a damper on the rest of the day's proceedings. When I get my list out that evening, I write down Fabio's name and what he did. I ask myself if I have any resentment. Did I harm him? I then look at where I was defective in character; was I selfish, self-seeking, dishonest, frightened or inconsiderate? I establish through this process whether I owe an amends (most of the time

I do) and make it on the phone straight away (if it is early enough to do so), or first thing in the morning. I then ask God to forgive me for hurting one of His creations, for not reflecting Jesus in my response, and I ask Him to restore His relationship with me.

Most of the time these days, I am able to do an inventory on the spot. As a typical real-life example: I finish my time of prayer, reading and meditation with God in the mornings at around 5.15am. I feel really positive and uplifted and have set it in my mind that I will not allow the drivers in the traffic to bother me on my way to work. I will continue speaking to the Lord during the day, and I will have a very peaceful day. Then, after being on the road less than five minutes, my old friend the taxi driver swerves in front of me and stops to pick someone up. Off goes my hooter, up goes the finger and verbal venom spews forth (a bit silly, seeing as he cannot hear me anyway – probably just as well). I feel devastated that all my resolve has gone out the window! The problem is just that; it's all *my* resolve. I made these wonderful "pie in the sky" plans of how peaceful I would be and completely left God out of it. I know I cannot be patient and peaceful on my own; only God has the power to do that in me. Straight away I say, "Lord, sorry for excluding You from my day. I cannot do anything without You. Once again in my dealings with this taxi driver, I was afraid and inconsiderate. Please forgive me and restore our relationship, in Jesus' name. Amen." I might go past the taxi driver and mouth the word "sorry" and give him a smile and the "thumbs up". I feel immediately at peace and my day is really not ruined. Sometimes I have to repeat this process several times during the course of the day in various scenarios, and it works each time.

This step may sound like a big deal and fuss, but it really works to set one at peace. The more you keep practising it, the more normal and easier it becomes. There will be times when the "madness" is on you, and you cannot do all of this. I can almost guarantee that you won't feel good, but do not let guilt get a hold of you. I find that guilt sucks the life out of a person. You will calm down and when you do, get to your inventory straight away. Go to God, make your amends with Him and the other person, and you will see how the peace returns to you. As I've said before, we are not perfect yet, we are striving towards perfection and God understands this. He loves us and He wants to renew our relationship with Him.

The action for Step 10

Download the Personal Inventory worksheet[50] or draw up a blank template on a piece of paper from my example on page 245.

Personal Inventory

1) Put your Step 10 Personal Inventory worksheet next to you and carefully go through my example on page 245 (as a prompt for during the day, you can make up a small prompt card with just the nine checks written on it from the Personal Inventory worksheet that you can laminate and carry with you in your wallet or pocket – I used to do this initially, until I knew them by heart. This way you can do an on-the-spot inventory if you have the

50. https://www.malcolmdown.co.uk/worksheets

temperament to do so at that moment.) Your main warning signs to prompt you to need to do your personal inventories is going to be internal pain or an uneasy discomfort. When you've had an interaction of any kind that has left you feeling pain, you will know that you played a part. Follow my explanation to my worksheet, *How I filled in the first entry on the Personal Inventory worksheet*, on page 243 to help give guidance.

2) Review your day, paying specific attention to situations and encounters that made you feel hurt, uncomfortable or down. Write each of them down in the first column.

3) Follow the *Personal Example of My Inventory Worksheet*. Read through my example and do the same for each of your listed people, institutions or principles. If an amends needs to be made, do so as soon as you possibly can.

4) Make sure to make amends to the Lord in prayer through Jesus Christ.

Your daily inventory shouldn't take more than ten minutes or so. As I have said before, this is something you will need to do sincerely each day, but it does become quite habitual after a while.

How I filled in the first entry on the Personal Inventory worksheet

Question

Do I have resentment?	Yes – he disobeyed the rules of the road and could have caused an accident and harm (I tick the box).
Have I harmed?	Yes – I verbally abused him (I tick the box).
Was I selfish?	No – This is not a selfish expectation.
Was I self-seeking?	Yes – I wanted him not to inconvenience me (I tick the box).
Was I dishonest?	No – there was no proper interaction.
Was I frightened?	Yes – very frightened as I nearly drove into him (I tick the box).
Was I inconsiderate?	Yes – I never considered anything of what might be going on in his life that may have caused him to do what he did (I tick the box).
Do I need to make amends?	No – it is impractical to do so in the middle of the traffic. If I could, I would say something like, "In my recent dealings with you, I was self-seeking, frightened and inconsiderate, and I might have harmed you with my verbal abuse. I just want to say that I am truly sorry for this."

I need to pray and meditate	Not optional, as I need to restore my relationship with God. I pray something like, "Dear heavenly Father, I come to You to confess that I have been self-seeking, frightened and inconsiderate, and this has led me to verbally abuse one of Your creations. I ask You to forgive me for possibly hurting that taxi driver, and I ask that You bless him with all the grace and blessings You give me. Lord, please heal his hurt, and I ask that You restore my relationship with You. I ask, Holy Spirit, for the guidance and strength to hand these shortcomings over to You, as I know I cannot change these things in myself; but You can. I ask this all in Jesus' name. Amen."

Example of My Personal Inventory Worksheet

Daily personal inventory	People, Institutions and Principles			
Checks	A. Taxi driver	B. Steel fixer	C. Municipality	D. My wife
1. Do I have resentment?	✓		✓	✓
2. Have I harmed?	✓	✓		✓
3. Was I selfish?				✓
4. Was I self-seeking?	✓	✓	✓	✓
5. Was I dishonest?			✓	
6. Was I frightened?	✓	✓		✓
7. Was I inconsiderate?	✓	✓	✓	✓
8. Do I need to make amends?		✓	✓	✓
9. I need to pray and meditate.	Done	Done	Done	Done

Step 11

We sought through prayer and meditation
to improve our conscious contact with
God, through Jesus Christ, praying only
for knowledge of His will for us, and the
power to carry that out.

(Spirituality)

*Let the words of my mouth, and the meditation of my
heart, be acceptable in thy sight, O LORD, my strength,
and my redeemer.*   Psalm 19:14

This step contains our most important mission on earth
and one that most people are no doubt striving to achieve
in some way or another, consciously or subconsciously.
This is to get to know God, and then to know Him better.
There is something inherent in our nature that has this
desire to know our creator. I was a person who ended up
looking for this connection in all the wrong places, but I was
most definitely looking, even if it was only a subconscious
searching of an equilibrium between my soul and my
Maker. This fits into the design of why we were created.
I've heard it said that God created man to be a companion.

That's a nice idea, but one should be careful here because this implies that God might have been bored or lonely or that He somehow lacked something. I understand that God is *complete* in every way and therefore needs nothing for fulfilment. Rather, I believe that God is love and we were created to be another expression of, and for His love. His perfect design for *all* of us is to love Him back. He wants us to have a relationship with Him, and any relationship requires contact of some kind. The more contact we have, the more meaningful and deep the relationship becomes. Because God is not a being we can see or hear, our main form of contact is through prayer and meditation. For me prayer is talking to God, while meditation is listening and thinking. However, I have found that the way God speaks to me most often is in His written Word – the Bible.

It is impossible to fully understand God's plans and ways. We have seen that as we are His creation, He knows best how we function and how to fulfil that function at the optimum level.

> *But as it is written, Eye hath not seen, nor ear heard, neither have entered into the heart of man, the things which God hath prepared for them that love him.*
>
> Paul quoting Isaiah in 1 Corinthians 2:9

So, to pray for what we think ourselves or others need, even if it seems good, is not always the best. This is why our safest bet is to pray for the *knowledge of God's will for us*. This is only the first step though, because it is all very well knowing something, but if we are incapable of executing the revealed plan of action, what good would that be? I had an acquaintance many years back now who was quite a charismatic speaker. One of the things he said often was,

"Knowledge is not power . . . *applied* knowledge is power." This is so true, as the apostle Paul knew what to do and yet he could not do it by his own strength; he needed God's help to apply it in his life.[51]

I once saw an accident happen at an intersection. Two cars smashed into each other; it was not serious and there were no injuries. I pulled to the side of the road and got out to see if anyone was hurt. There were cars trying to turn but were obstructed by these two vehicles, and the oncoming drivers were not helping because they were slowing down to have a good look. I thought I'd help by stopping some traffic and waving other traffic on, but no one took any notice of me. It wasn't long before there was total chaos and I decided to slink off. Just then, a tow truck arrived on the scene and two men jumped out. One went to the accident and started making arrangements with the drivers. The other, who was wearing a Hi-Viz vest, walked to the middle of the intersection and started sorting out the traffic. I watched in fascination as he said a few calm words to one or two of the drivers and then started directing traffic. Within a few minutes the traffic was flowing again, and the smashed cars were towed off. I got back into the car with my pride in tatters, wondering how he had managed to get right precisely what I had tried to achieve just a little while earlier. He was no policeman and yet the drivers listened to him where they had ignored me. As I drove off, it dawned on me that the Hi-Viz vest the man was wearing had given him the power that I had lacked.

You see, despite all my knowledge and quick thinking, my effort was worthless because I never had the power

51. See Romans 7:14-25.

backing me. So, when we ask for *knowledge of His will for us,* we ask too for God to give us the power to follow through with His plan. The power needed in any given situation can come in many different ways, and I found that it is better for me not to know in which way it would come, so that it would stop me trying to tweak or interfere with that plan. All I know is that when His will is done, I feel joy, peace and comfort within myself. For interest's sake, I believe the power comes mainly in the form of the fruit of the Spirit.

> *But the fruit of the Spirit is love, joy, peace, patience, kindness, goodness, faithfulness, gentleness, self-control; against such things there is no law.*
>
> Galatians 5:22-23 (ESV)

I know that when I get through the day successfully, it is due to the power of God, and I thank Him. Every now and again, normally in my daily time with God, He opens my eyes to the kindness I might have exercised in a situation that led to its successful conclusion, and I smile and thank Him for being my God. Moments of realization like these do not happen all the time to me, but they do give me a glimpse of what it must be like to be in continual relationship with God.

I would briefly like to share my experience with *prayer, reading* and *meditating.* I now understood that I was to start praying on a regular basis with the intention of forming a closer relationship with God. Some may ask why it needs to be through Jesus Christ, and some may think it a bit formal when they see that all my prayers in this book end, "... in Jesus' name. Amen." The Bible tells us:

Jesus saith unto him, I am the way, the truth, and the life: no man cometh unto the Father, but by me.

John 14:6

So that is what I do. I remember sitting with my mentor/ sponsor at this time and asking him what the right way would be to pray. He smiled and told me the Bible had my answer, because Jesus answered that exact same question asked by His disciples in Luke 11:1-4 and Matthew 6:9-13. So, I took the prayer Jesus gave them and I have never looked back; I still pray it today. I have modified it a little, not in its meaning but in its "lingo". My prayer now goes:

"Dear heavenly Father, Holy is Your name. Your kingdom come, Your will be done, on earth as it is in heaven. Give me today my daily bread, both physically as I eat what You have provided, and spiritually as I read Your Word and am taught by Your Holy Spirit. Forgive me my sins and trespasses [I name the ones I remember], as I forgive those who have trespassed against me [once again, I name the ones I remember]. Lead me not into temptation of any sorts, but deliver me from evil, especially the evils of self, ego and pride, and the evil of not trusting You. For Yours is the kingdom, the power, and the glory, forever and ever. In Jesus' name. Amen."

This is the way I interpret the prayer, and I believe it says everything that needs to be said to God. Firstly, we acknowledge God as our Father, but also show Him reverence by remembering His holiness. Secondly, we show our hope for God's ultimate plan, and submit our will to His will, which is essential, as I have previously explained. Thirdly, we are going to God for our needs both physical and spiritual, we are not taking our wants to Him. Fourthly, we are making relationship restitution with God and with our fellow man. Fifthly, we are asking God's protection against things over which we are powerless and we are asking Him to cleanse our souls. Lastly, and I believe most importantly, we are acknowledging God as the supreme creator of the universe, recognizing His omnipotence, and giving Him all the glory, which is rightfully His – this is our true purpose.

When I first started working the Program, I found that my concentration and patience levels were at an all-time low. By the time I had reached Step 11, I found these levels had improved but they were still not where they should be. I found I could only tackle tasks in short spells before my concentration would waver. My mentor had suggested reading a chapter from the Bible every morning. It is strange how quickly a person becomes estranged from things that once were second nature, but I found myself floundering, not knowing where to start reading or how to read. Did I read an entire chapter? Should I take notes . . . ? It was all too much for me to handle and I found myself slipping into despair.

It is amazing how God works, and I overheard someone say in a conversation to another, "It does not matter with the things of God how much one does or how often you get it wrong; what matters is trying to maintain consistency, even if it is little by little." I remembered it said years ago that the best place to start reading in the Bible is the Gospels, so I started reading from the beginning of the New Testament. I set aside the idea of trying to read an entire chapter or writing anything down and set myself the task of praying the Lord's Prayer and reading one *verse* a day. After reading the verse, I asked God to show me what He wanted me to see and understand, and then went to bed. The whole exercise would take me less than three minutes but I resolved to be diligent and, come hell or high water, I was going to do this *every day*.

I want to leave it at that and move on to today. My reading, praying and meditating has taken on a life of its own with the Holy Spirit as the director. I read more, pray longer, and find myself in my thoughts with God sometimes for hours. In my mind my resolve is still to read something from the Bible and to speak to God every day. I feel now that I cannot miss one day without speaking to my God, Father and Friend – it's such a beautiful thing.

I have never particularly liked the word "meditation"; it always seemed so long, so adult, so boring . . . I guess we all have our ways and styles, but my understanding of meditation is quite rudimentary. To me, it is just thinking and listening to thoughts that come to you during a conscious time set aside with God. I often find my thoughts drift off to my worries or to my dreams. Before, I used to fight it and think I must be focused on God. Now I see it differently and it brings me a lot of peace and joy. What I do is ask the Holy Spirit to be with me in my thoughts and to speak to me. Thereafter, I let my mind flow and enjoy. I might drift off into a concern about a work issue. I go through the issue and how it makes me feel and how I could handle it. Often resentment wants to spring up, and I go through a quick Step 10. I then ask if my approach would actually work and try to think what I might need to change to make it work. Usually, an idea comes to me that makes sense, and I take that as God speaking to me through the Holy Spirit. Many times, it is an untested approach, and I go and apply it. I find it such fun to see how the whole scenario unfolds for the good; it truly is remarkable. If I find my thoughts wander to my dreams, I let them play out and enjoy them. After my thoughts have drifted a while, I stop and look at where the Lord is in all this, and I find that He is everywhere. I find I have come to use a godlier approach towards work issues, and I see how God has shifted my dreams and visions towards being of benefit to others. It is in times like these that a certain beautiful scripture really becomes a reality in my life:

Even the mystery which hath been hid from ages and from generations, but now is made manifest to his saints: To whom God would make known what is the riches of the glory of this mystery among the Gentiles; which is Christ in you, the hope of glory...

Colossians 1:26-27

This is what meditation is for me; it's wrapped up in reading God's Word, speaking to Him, listening to Him, sharing things with Him – and it is not boring. When I do all these things, I experience exactly what the lyrics of that old song, written by Helen H. Lemmel in 1922, say:

Turn your eyes upon Jesus.
Look full in His wonderful face.
And the things of the earth will grow strangely dim,
In the light of His glory and grace.
Amen.

Finally, as part of my getting to know God, I came to see my need to join a church. This may come across as a bit cliché, but it had been a sore point for me in the past. However, I have come to realize that a coal taken out of the fire does not stay hot. There are so many people we can love (doing things for them that they need done, for free and fun), and so much encouragement that we need, that we cannot bypass this part. There is no stronger motivation for me than simple obedience to God's Word.

And let us not give up meeting together. Some are in the habit of doing this. Instead, let us encourage one another with words of hope. Let us do this even more as you see Christ's return approaching.

Hebrews 10:25 (NIRV)

For me, it is an instruction, and I cannot live up to His glory without going to church. I know God delights in it, and the thought of His delighting in something that I can do gives me joy. There is a beautiful scripture in Jeremiah that sums up the importance of this step:

Thus saith the Lord, Let not the wise man glory in his wisdom, neither let the mighty man glory in his might, let not the rich man glory in his riches: But let him that glorieth glory in this, that he understandeth and knoweth me, that I am the LORD which exercise lovingkindness, judgment, and righteousness, in the earth: for in these things I delight, saith the LORD.

Jeremiah 9:23-24

The action for Step 11

1) Make a definite time in the morning or evening, or both, for five uninterrupted minutes.

2) Start off by saying the Lord's Prayer – think of the meaning of the words as you pray.

   "Our Father, who art in heaven; hallowed be Thy Name. Thy kingdom come, Thy will be done, on earth as it is in heaven. Give us today our daily bread, and forgive us our trespasses, as we forgive those who trespass against us. Lead us not into temptation but deliver us from evil. For Thine is the kingdom, the power, and the glory, forever and ever. Amen."

3) If you find that someone or something comes to mind, you can pray for them as well; it is good to pray for other people. If you have your own prayer, then you can pray that instead of (or in addition to) the Lord's Prayer. You may want to thank Him for another day He has given you, as well as the things you have that you are grateful for. I also suggest you ask God for the ability to surrender your will/plans/desires over to Him, and that instead, ask that He grant you the knowledge of *His* will for your life, and the power needed to carry it out.

4) Before you start reading the Bible you might say a short prayer like:

   "Dear heavenly Father, as I read Your Word, please reveal through Your Holy Spirit exactly what I need to see and apply in my life. In Jesus' name. Amen."

5) Open your Bible to the New Testament and start reading from the beginning, one verse a day. If you feel like reading more, do so. My only advice is not to read yourself into exhaustion, because it will kill your resolve to read every day and you might start missing days. When you have read up to the last book of the Bible, Revelation, I recommend you either start the New Testament again or move to the Old Testament. I suggest you do not read Revelation until you are stronger; it can be quite confusing and hard to understand for someone starting on a road to a relationship with the Lord.

6) Try to meditate; just think of whatever comes to mind, with the understanding that God is present and in conversation with you while you do so. I believe your experience will be unique, do whatever you feel comes naturally to you. For example, you might walk, drive, lie down or sing. Try to see how this all fits in with God, include Him in your thoughts and plans. Do not get too stressed about this. I find it has a life of its own and God will find His way with you. Relax and enjoy; whether you feel it or not, you are actually getting into closer contact with God.

7) Please remember that this is just a start; I do not need to say anymore. If you are sincere, your relationship will grow and form on its own.

8) If you are not in a church, pray and ask God to lead you to a church He would like you to be part of. If you struggle, just bear in mind that you are there out of obedience to Him and because you

are building a relationship with Him. Try to get involved where you can, even if it feels strange; the Lord will help you. If you are in a church, may I encourage you to see if there are areas where you may be able to get involved. I used to ask the Lord to help me keep a firm attitude of wanting to help others, as unto Him.

Step 12

Having had a spiritual awakening as
the result of these steps, we tried to carry
this message to others, and practise
these principles in all our affairs.

(Service)

*Brethren, if a man be overtaken in a fault, ye which are
spiritual, restore such an one in the spirit of meekness;
considering thyself, lest thou also be tempted. Bear ye
one another's burdens, and so fulfil the law of Christ.*

Galatians 6:1-2

This step starts off by talking about something I'd never
heard of before. The closest I'd come to any kind of
"awakening" was a rude awakening; like sticking my head
out the bedroom window after a night out, only to see
my car had been "modified" somewhat. I had heard of a
"spiritual experience", though I never understood it. I have
subsequently had a few spiritual experiences, which I
count as a touch of love and reassurance from God, not
something I experience every day.

One such experience I can remember vividly. I was in
church, and we were singing a song in which some of

the words were, "Holy, Holy are You, Lord God Almighty; worthy is the Lamb, worthy is the Lamb; You are Holy."[52] I was singing along when all of a sudden, I got a powerful sense of how awesome and majestic God is, and of how He still had time to think of me and change my life. Now you can ask my wife or anyone that knows me, I am not a tearful person, but tears ran down my cheeks as I felt God's love. It was a most incredible experience, and I left the church feeling warm and content inside for days.

The spiritual *awakening* referred to in Step 12 was nothing like that experience for me. It seemed to come as a natural result of the first 11 steps.

I have heard of people having spiritual awakenings without the steps but have only actually met one such person. For me, it was a gradual process and was only really realized properly when I had completed Step 9. By the time I had reached Step 12, my awakening had grown, and I find that it is still growing, and this is part of the new journey. You realize that you are on a journey here on earth, and that you need to keep growing.

I found that I no longer needed to lean on my own understanding, and that I was able to trust the Lord more, even if it felt strange at first. My mind became more and more preoccupied with God's things (usually centred on helping others) and this gave me the sense of ease and comfort, which other dependencies had temporarily given me in the past. The difference was that this sense of ease and comfort came without harming others or myself. In fact, my whole attitude was now one of "What can I do for

---

52. Agnus Dei

another?" instead of "What can I get from another?" There have been many that I have shared my story with who had wanted what God had so freely given me, but they were not prepared to work through the steps as suggested. They could not, therefore, receive this gift – this spiritual awakening.

God cannot deal with any areas of our lives where we are still in charge, we have to surrender this *right* to Him. It is because we have *been in the way* and had not even realized it that we have not had this spiritual awakening before. Because we battle self, ego and pride, we cannot see these things and could not stand aside, even if we wanted to. This is why we need to work through the steps. The spiritual awakening began for me as the understanding started to properly sink in that God was now in control of my life. It was a clear realization that He was doing for me the things that I could not do for myself all along. However, I truly believe that a spiritual awakening is the onset of the realization that God is actually with me, in me, and that He has been approachable and caring of me the whole time.

If you are at this step and have an inner sense of hope, peace or comfort despite other things going on in your life, I put it to you that you are already experiencing a spiritual awakening. You could be experiencing no other difference whatsoever. For each person it is different; some say that they feel totally different inside. However you may see it, you will sense a difference, even if it is an underlying hope or excitement that something unique is going to happen. Whether you realize it or not is irrelevant; God's power, which you lacked before, is now in full control.

Now that we have had a spiritual awakening we are not to rest on our laurels; we have something God wants us to *do*. The first thing this step instructs us to do is to try to carry this message to others. I am glad this step uses the word "tried" here, because people generally have their own agendas and they are not always ready to hear our wonderful tidings of peace, joy and comfort. Some are eager, but the *work* is too much. To be completely honest, I don't have a clue as to who, when, how or if anyone will listen to and apply the Program.

I'd like to share one of my first experiences of "carrying the message" with you. I believe that our experiences shared are the best witness of how we came into a real relationship with God and, as such, I am sharing a story of another alcoholic. This fella was of Danish descent, and he must have been about eight years older than me; I shall call him Michael. I had been about a year sober at the time, and I was really enjoying following the Program and going to all the meetings. Michael came up to me after one of the Margate meetings and asked if I would be his sponsor. He explained that he liked what I had shared and could relate it to quite a few things in his life. I was happy someone had asked me to help them, and so I set up a meeting with him three days later, on the Thursday evening. When I arrived, he was sitting outside at a wire-mesh patio table set. I remember thinking how the presence of the two-litre glass bottle of Old Brown Sherry in the middle of the rickety wire table made the two crystal scotch glasses look tiny and out of place. I should have left then; my sponsor had always said I should never play nursemaid or companion to a man while he was drinking. Anyway, he seemed to be able to string a coherent sentence together, so I sat down to hear his tales of woe. He told me how his mother had died seven years ago, how his girlfriend had left him many years previously, and how he was all alone. I tried to tell him my story and how I'd found companionship at the meetings, and that he should join in. Truth be told, though, he wasn't interested in all that and kept trying to get me to have a drink, which I obviously kept refusing. It dawned on me after an hour or so that he wanted someone to sit and talk nonsense to while he drank. I made a polite excuse and left.

Thereafter, every other day I'd get calls from Michael in various stages of inebriation. Each time I told him that I'd be happy to come and see him but only when he was sober and not drinking. There was a stint of about four days during which I heard nothing from him, and he wasn't answering my calls. I thought at first that he may be upset with me, but something said I should go to his place and check on him – I believe it was the Lord. I found him on the bed, locked in his house, and he wasn't moving. I shouted to him through the burglar bars, but he wouldn't budge. I got the police out and they broke open the bars and called an ambulance. One of the paramedics said that if he had been found a day later, he would have been dead from alcohol poisoning. The police also found a loaded .22 pistol on the bed next to him.

They admitted him to the Port Shepstone government hospital for severe dehydration. The police took his .22 and said I should tell him they had it when he got out. He was in hospital for three weeks and I played the Good Samaritan, bringing him cigarettes, toiletries, clothes, and visiting him once a day. In the beginning he had really bad amnesia and kept asking me to tell his mother where he was. I shared my story of recovery with him in that time, and I was just really chuffed to be of service.

When he came out, I took him to meetings with me, and he would share how he had nearly died and how well he was doing now. I felt great; I had been able to pass on the message and someone else had recovered. He started driving again, the police gave him his pistol back, and he even got his job back as a security patrolman. After about three months, though, I started noticing he was coming to fewer and fewer meetings, and he wasn't calling as often. I tried to phone him a few times, but his phone was always off. I called round his place one afternoon, and the other tenants said he'd moved out overnight a few weeks back. About a month later I found out that he had been found dead in Southport; he had shot himself.

I was devastated, angry and upset all at the same time. I got a hold of Blackie (he used to patrol the Transkei coastline in the police force and his skin got so dark from the sun that that was where he got his nickname from), who was one of my Christian sponsors. He had a high-pitched slow chuckle, and when I told him that I would never help anyone again because it doesn't work, he just sat back and gave off one of his long whining chuckles. Once he had caught his breath, he said (in his very Afrikaans accent); "Rory . . . stop trying to play God."

There is another story I'd like to share. I used to go to the local supermarket in Port Shepstone. There was this toothless inebriate, a homeless chap who often came to harass me for money or takeaway. He would refuse food I bought from the supermarket but used to ask if I had money for him, or if I would buy him takeaway food – I never gave him either. He was a drunk of what I then considered the hopeless variety, surviving on methylated spirits and any drug available. But one day I offered to take him to a meeting with me if he wanted to get sober. (If something stirs inside my heart that I know goes against my general nature, it is usually the Holy Spirit.) He said he would like to go, and I picked him up two days later. He was as pickled as a cucumber when I fetched him, but nevertheless off we went to the meeting.

At the meeting he kept disrupting proceedings, and I asked another fella to take over while I took him outside. He started swearing and said that everyone looked down on him and that all he wanted was a cigarette. I managed to get him a cigarette from a night watchman at the church, and said that I didn't look down on him, and that I had felt the same as he did before. I told him that no matter what, I knew God loved Him just as he was right now. He broke down in tears and apologized. That night I booked him into a shelter for the homeless.

The next day I got him into a two-week rehabilitation centre in Durban, where he went through the 12-step Program extensively and, when he came out, I got him into a redevelopment programme in Amanzimtoti. They had a church there, which he attended a few times a week, they fed and clothed him, and they started teaching him skills in hydroponics – the boy flourished! He even got a new set of "gnashers", of which he was very proud. I hooked him up with a mobile phone and he used to let me know how things were going from time to time.

A year later he wrote down his story and sent it to me and my heart was warmed. I went back to my sponsor Blackie, to give him the good news of how well this guy had done, and how proud I was of everything. He looked at me and gave me another one of those long whining chuckles, and his words were exactly the same: "Rory . . . stop trying to play God."

Right at that moment the penny dropped. I had the most incredible clarification that could only have been a revelation from the Lord. I was not responsible for failure in someone's life, nor was I responsible for success in their life. My sole purpose was to be the conduit to convey the message and power, nothing more. Blackie was famous for a saying that I use all the time today: "Just for today, I want to help someone, but the big secret is, nobody must know about it." This whole lesson ties so well into what Chuck C said in one of his talks at the Pala Mesa retreat in 1975:

To be good for nothing, this is the freedom of life.

In other words, we are good in return for nothing at all. Our sole motivation is to pass on to others what we have so freely received – *for nothing in return*.

This *nothing* actually includes any expected results. But if that is the case, why would we do it, it seems ludicrous!? Here's where God's real plan comes in. We saw in Step 11 that our main purpose is to have a relationship with God and to show Him we love Him. The best demonstration of love we can give God is to obey Him,[53] and this means to try to help others as we've been helped. There are two scriptures which tell us this clearly:

Who comforteth us in all our tribulation, that we may be able to comfort them which are in any trouble, by the comfort wherewith we ourselves are comforted of God.   2 Corinthians 1:4

---

53. See 1 Samuel 15:22.

Heal the sick, cleanse the lepers, raise the dead, cast out devils: freely ye have received, freely give.

Matthew 10:8

(Notice the words "any trouble" in the first verse.)

It is really that simple. The big question we may ask is why bother if their wellbeing does not depend on us and often, because God has given people free will, it doesn't depend on Him either? God's Holy Spirit can reveal the truth to people, but the ultimate decision lies with them. It is amazing but in the face of all evidence people often still choose the path of destruction. The reason we continue to pass the message on is that we are showing God our gratitude, and by working with others for God's great purpose, it keeps us in a relationship with Him. I know He doesn't need us to help Him, but I love the fact that He wants us with Him, right next to Him in His mission of "bringing many sons to glory"[54] – that's what it's all about. Two oxen in a yoke are side by side, on the same mission, and that's where He wants us.

Take my yoke upon you, and learn of me; for I am meek and lowly in heart: and ye shall find rest unto your souls. For my yoke is easy, and my burden is light.

Matthew 11:29-30

Once we have this mindset, the rest is easy. I pray in the morning and ask God to show me *anybody* who needs help with anything, and when they come along, I try to help them. It can take a while sometimes before God brings a person across your path, but in the meantime why not try

---

54. Hebrews 2:10.

whatever you can; prepare the lunch, clean a colleague's workstation, pick up a piece of litter – do whatever, because you'll feel great. I often remind myself that I am doing it for God, because of what He does for me and because I love Him.

If you meet someone who wants to know how to experience intimacy in relationship with God, you should be glad because this is the Holy Spirit calling *you* into a deeper relationship with God. Relax, because it is going to be so simple to help someone, as God will be doing all the work. What you will need is patience and time, and you will need to ask the Lord for that. I am going to suggest the entire process of helping someone in one sentence; are you ready for it?

You will pray for their need, get them to read through the book (or you could read through it together with them), and be there when they do the "Working" part of each step to give prompts, guidance and maybe listen to their Step 5.

I do suggest you get another copy of this book for them to work through with you. This process is all I have ever done with those I've sponsored and mentored. If they fall away, it's okay; some come back, and some never do, but that is not your responsibility. I can promise you this though, as you try to help someone your relationship with God will keep growing into something more wonderful each day.

The last thing we try to do in this final step of the Program is to "practise these principles in all of our affairs". Which principles are we talking about, and just exactly what is meant by "all affairs"? This one I am pleased to say the Holy Spirit showed me personally and I was able to put it directly into practice. The principles we are talking about are the principles in this recovery Program as laid out in these 12 steps. For me, "all affairs" meant literally everything that affected me in my life, from small to large, and from people to institutions to principles.

This is a vital aspect in breaking through into a sincere intimate relationship with our heavenly Father. Remember, the first sin ever committed was by Satan (the devil), and it was the sin of self, ego – pride:

How art thou fallen from heaven, O Lucifer [Satan], son of the morning! how art thou cut down to the ground, which didst weaken the nations! For thou hast said in thine heart, I will ascend into heaven, I will exalt my throne above the stars of God: I will sit also upon the mount of the congregation, in the sides of the north: I will ascend above the heights of the clouds; I will be like the most High. Yet thou shalt be brought down to hell, to the sides of the pit. Isaiah 14:12-15

As we have seen, the sin we are most guilty of is just this: self, ego – pride. As I've said many times previously, what makes this sin so deadly is that if we have it, we cannot see it in ourselves at all. How do you rid yourself of something you don't believe you have? I find the Lord uses pain, and this is a good indication of something not being right in us. Once we feel this pain or uneasiness, we can then practise these principles – the 12 steps.

I had a terrible underlying fear of not having enough money to live, a sense of economic insecurity if you will. In 2008 the worldwide economic recession hit the Natal South Coast but, just before it did, business had been booming and people were making fortunes, especially in the building industry, and I was on the bandwagon for sure. I was building holiday homes and complexes for a company and was doing a bit of speculation of my own. To give you an idea of the magnitude of the situation, in a coastal stretch of about 30 miles there were 64 individual estate agencies. If you could talk, you could sell. When the economic recession hit globally, it had a huge and almost instantaneous impact on the property market on the Natal South Coast. People stopped buying immediately, as this was surplus money they had been using on holiday homes. I had bought a house in Margate and was in the process of dividing the land and also getting plans passed for building a second house. It was then that the recession hit, and I found I could not sell the house or the separated plot of land. The building of the second house was dependent on the sale of the existing house, and so there I was stuck between a rock and a hard place. I then made an exceedingly poor decision. Instead of selling up for what I could get and making arrangements with the bank to pay off the balance, I tried to hold out by obtaining overdrafts, loans and credit cards to service the mortgage repayments and get my plans passed for the second house. The long and the short of it was that I was stuck in a combined debt of about R1.6 million.[55] On top of this, work was as scarce as hen's teeth down there and that, combined with the fact that the company I was working for might not be able to keep me on, really started haunting me.

I got married at the end of May 2009, and this also compounded my financial woes (this "woe", however,

---

55. Roughly equivalent to £100,000 or US$130,000, although as I was dealing in assets, it was more like owing £200,000 or US$250,000.

I wouldn't change for the world!). I cannot begin to describe the raw fear that crept into me, and I had to face it sober. "What am I to do?" was my cry.

I went and saw a debt counsellor and went under debt review. This left us scraping the barrel, and "pap 'n' wors" (stiff corn porridge and South African farmer sausage) became our staple diet, as there was no money for anything else. I went to my sponsor with a plea for help. His first comment was, "Sorry, my Boet (Brother)," and then he gave me two pearls of wisdom from Step 7 and Step 12, which I had read over and over before but had never put to use. He said, "Rory, you have to go to God, and you should do the Program with that fear of yours."

I went to God every morning with my fear, and I replaced the word "ourselves" in Step 1 with the word "fear", so that it read, "We admitted we were powerless over *fear* – that our lives had become unmanageable." I went through the 12 steps of the Program with fear as the focal point of my powerlessness and unmanageability. Although working the Program and taking my fear to God helped me get through each day and night, this fear did not leave me for quite a while.

Eventually the inevitable happened and I had to look for other work. I got a job with a construction company in Pretoria (500 miles inland from where we were), and I had to leave the family down on the coast for two months while I went to work. The fear gripped me night after night in such a way that I'd wake up sweating in the middle of the night, with my stomach in a knot. I would sometimes just pray repeatedly, or I'd get up and sing hymns and choruses. Then the fear would subside, and I'd sleep.

Monday mornings were the worst. I'd wake up early with that "knot" and just ask God to help me through the day and week – and He would.

My wife Pauline, who worked for a bank, got a transfer and moved up to Pretoria, but the fear still persisted. I kept taking it back to the beginning of the Program and going through it again and again. That December I was docked half my pay. When I inquired, I was told that I was only entitled to six days' leave instead of eighteen because I'd started in August. They have what they call a builders' shutdown in South Africa, which meant the three weeks I was off was forced leave, and therefore it was illegal for a company to take it as unpaid leave. I took it to God instead of arbitration, and although Pauline and I could only stay at home and were unable to buy Christmas presents for the family, we paid the bills and we spent one of the most meaningful and intimate periods of our lives together – this is the power of God at work.

My financial situation got to the point where I could not keep up payments. The general standard of living was much higher in Pretoria, and my current net salary was a bit less than what I had been earning down on the South Coast. The fear kept coming, and I went to a friend who suggested an attorney who could possibly help with a sequestration.[56] I went and saw the attorney, and he said that sequestration was the best option available to me, but there were a few concerns. One of them was that I could not sequestrate until all my property assets were sold. I was advised to continue all payments, sell what I could for whatever I could get, and wait. It was a long and complicated process.

---

56. Declaring Insolvency.

Over a year passed and the situation had become critical. I had understood that I would be able to sequestrate after a further two months, but then the attorney came back to me and told me that he was concerned about one financial institution being able to oppose the court order and demand payment in the region of R180,000.[57]

It was at this point that another miracle happened in my life. One of those mornings I woke up and the fear was gone. Somehow, I just knew that no matter what happened we would be taken care of, it was incredible! After six-and-a-half years of taking this fear to God and working it through the Program, it was gone – just like that. I did not know whether I would be able to be sequestrated, whether an institution would oppose anything, or whether all my debt would be written off or not. But I had freedom from the fear.

It turned out well and I have since been cleared of all debt. My job changed, and I started to earn double what I had before. Pauline was promoted, and her salary increased as well. We were able to buy a car and a house in her name, and God has continued to look after us and bless us both.

Through this experience I learned that God had to remove the fear before He changed my circumstances, otherwise I would feel fear every time my financial situation changed slightly for the worse. Now I know I will be looked after no matter what happens. I got through fear one day at a time with God's help and working the Program for six-and-a-half years, and the thing that was different from anything else before, was that *I knew that I knew,* deep down inside,

---

57. Approximately £10,000 or $12,000.

that He would help me this time. The reason I knew this so emphatically was because He had removed the desire to drink from me in an instant, and in my mind that was a far larger problem than not having enough money.

To date I still battle constantly with a foul mouth and a grumpy temper, and I take it to God through the Program every day. This time *I know* that He will remove this problem as well in time, because it is a lot smaller than fear, and it took time for that defect to be removed.

After a year of sobriety I took smoking through the Program with God's help, and that desire left me as well. There are countless other victories and each one of them has been achieved through the same process. Only the time taken for the victory has differed. I often wondered why God could not remove them all in one fell swoop . . . I think one reason is that we are standing with our pride and ego in front of these individual "strongholds", and in some instances, I believe we are more stubborn and less desperate than at other times. But maybe the more important reason is that God is our Father, and He loves spending time with His children. Unfortunately, a lot of us become too "busy" for Him when all's well in our lives . . .

The action for Step 12

1) Sit back and take some time to think about your spiritual awakening. If you've come this far in working through the steps and you sense a change in yourself, maybe it's only a subtle sense of hope or ease and comfort, I would say that you have had

a spiritual awakening, regardless of how you may feel otherwise.

If you've come this far and you are feeling exactly the same, I would be surprised, but it is not impossible. In this instance my recommendation is to pray and ask God for an honest desire to willingly redo the Program with an open-mindedness that will allow God to change your life in any way He chooses – that His will be done. I would then, as I did with my "lack of money" fear, go back and redo the Program. Try to be thorough, and if you know that there is something you cannot do, ask God to give you the stamina to persist until you overcome the problem. You will find it a lot quicker this time, as most of your inventory is done. I know this suggestion may make you feel like you are losing the will to live if you have to go through the Program again, but ask God for the strength, and when you get to it, it may be the smallest revelation that makes it all click into place. I believe that showing God your willingness and sincerity is something that He will always honour in your life (remember Jacob wrestling the angel and not letting go until the angel had given him a blessing . . .?)[58]

2) Each morning before you get up, pray and ask God for an opportunity to help somebody. It can be anyone and under any circumstances. My sponsor suggested a prayer, which I have mentioned previously and which you might use. It is very simple:

58. See Genesis 32:22-32.

"Dear heavenly Father, just for today I want to help someone. Please help me be reminded that the big secret is that nobody else must know about it. In Jesus' name. Amen."

3) I suggest helping anyone with anything that is within your capability to do, without disrupting your important commitments. You cannot take off a day's work to help someone move house for instance, unless you can do so in the proper way, i.e. request a day's leave that is due to you, in advance. God will guide you.

4) If you get a chance to share your story/experience/ testimony with anyone, do so. It is amazing how the Holy Spirit works in the heart of somebody when we share freely.

If you meet a person who shares that they do not really feel the presence of God in a real way (or anything along those lines), and is *asking for help*, set up a time with them at your place or at a neutral venue, and commence telling them your story. They may not actually have asked for help, which is why sharing your story is not advising or suggesting anything, but in sharing your struggles you had until you got introduced to a workable solution that has since brought you into a sincere and intimate relationship with God, they may of themselves relate to something in the story, and this may prompt them to ask. An example of how one would share one's story can be found on page 25 (the "My Miracle" story). If he or she wants to talk, then listen carefully. Their sharing often gives good insight into their particular situation. I don't want to say too much more on what one should do, because I believe that each situation is unique, and I believe in the power of the Holy Spirit to lead and guide you.

5) If, after you have shared your story, they show an interest in the solution of the Program, I suggest taking them through this book. You could recommend they get a copy, or you can let them read yours. When they come to the steps in the book you can meet up and go through each step together. You can even sit and read the book together from the beginning. As you do this, I recommend that you share your experiences with them and allow them to do the same. This is what I do when I show someone how the Program worked for me, and God through His Holy Spirit does the rest. Remember that we have no more power over the other person's relationship with God than we had over our own. The power must come from God, we are only vessels. Do not think it silly to take someone through the book, as it will continually enrich your walk with God and might provide just the right encouragement they need at that time.

6) If the person is looking for help but does not want to sit with you, suggest they get a copy of the book and go through it on their own. I have specifically tried to write it in such a way that the person can do the Program on their own should they choose to. As God begins to work in their hearts, so they

will open up to the right people at the right time –
be ready for God to use you again.

7) Once you are working with someone, suggest they
come to church with you or join one near where
they live. If they are in one already then encourage
them to continue and to get involved in helping
at their church, and joining a home group or Bible
study.

8) If the person you are working with is not a Christian,
just continue with the book and Program as if they
were; they will ask the appropriate questions when
the Holy Spirit prompts them. If they say they
are not a Christian, ask them if they would like to
become one. If they say yes, take them through the
sinner's prayer:

a. Ask them if they believe that Jesus Christ
came down to earth and that He died on the
cross for their sins.

b. Ask them then if they believe that God raised
Him from the dead.

c. Then finally ask them if they are willing to
repent and turn away from their old ways.

If they say yes to all of these, lead them through
this simple prayer, asking them to repeat after you
(or, if you are reading this book on your own, say
this prayer aloud):

"God, I believe that You sent Your Son Jesus to
earth and that He died on the cross for my sins.
I believe that You then raised Him from the dead

and that He is seated on Your right-hand side in heaven. I now repent of my old sinful ways, and I choose to follow You. In Jesus' name. Amen."

According to Romans 10:9, they/you have entered salvation and are now a child of God.

Very important: if the person you are helping is showing signs of illness (either mental or physical), do not try to solve that. We are not professionals, and you could do more harm than good. Rather, suggest a rehabilitation centre, doctor, psychiatrist or whatever you feel the Holy Spirit is showing you.

9) To practise these principles in all our affairs is to take each of our pains, problems and hindrances through the steps one at a time. You will find, though, that the lengthy work done in Steps 4, 5, 8 and 9 will be considerably shorter as time goes on. You will probably go through the steps in no more than a few hours. Most important is to recognize the defect of character as a sin, whether it was caused by you or not. You will right the wrong and you will try to help others. You may need to do this as part of your daily routine, as I did, for many years. Try not to lose heart, and try never to excuse sin, no matter what. God's Word says He will forgive your sins as often as you ask Him,[59] but nowhere does He say He will excuse our sins. As you experience victory over one sin, another may come up as the Holy Spirit deals with our unrighteousness and moves us ever closer to sanctification and right standing with God. Amen.

---

59. See 1 John 1:9 and Matthew 18:21-22.

PART THREE

Maintaining Relationship

Anne's Story

I was baptised as an adult at my local church in 2008. I contributed to church life and held roles of deaconship for a few years, and loved working with children in particular.

However, I became more and more despondent and frustrated in 2018–2019, culminating with me and my family leaving our spiritual home. We joined the Church of Jesus Christ of Latter-day Saints (LDS) and were baptised there within three months of joining, around September 2019. I loved some of the family groups, women's relief society and the adult-style Sunday school, and it seemed to be what we had been looking for. By March 2020, things started to get more pressured and discussions on God and Jesus became strange and I knew that this was not right. Both my husband and I felt uncomfortable with the direction and discussion on who God was.

We realized that we had made a big mistake and the impact was particularly felt by our children. For myself, I no longer really heard from God or felt the Holy Spirit during services, etc.

We prayed and realized we needed to go back to our church where we had been. We made it to the last service just before the first Covid lockdown, which was towards the end of March 2020. I was elated to be back, and we were welcomed with hugs, kisses and prayers, but most of all with love. It dawned on me that our church family loved us, had been praying for us, and had missed us. I felt sad that I had hurt them and not listened to their warnings and that I had argued with them. I was so sure I had been right in my decisions, but now I felt that I had egg on my face.

We spent the next year as a couple working with the elders face to face when restrictions allowed, but mainly on phone calls, Zoom meetings and texts to undo some of the things we had been exposed to, such as false teaching, unlearning harmful doctrine and replacing it with truth – using the Bible as the plumb line of this truth. Trying to renew my mind was hard and we were desperate to be brought back into membership, as we had officially left the LDS church. I was trying to find my way back to God – the real God – to truth and relationship with Him. Part way through this journey of renewing and learning, we were invited to join the "Entering into a deeper relationship with God" group run by Rory and his wife Pauline.

Apprehensively I joined with my husband and a small group of other people from church, because, as I said, I was really seeking a real and intimate relationship with God. I wasn't sure what to expect or if it was for me, but I knew I needed to get rid of the bad habits and traits I had picked up and to connect properly with God. I had a sense of God telling us to come home. The group provided fellowship on a small scale, which was what we needed too.

The first few steps took some hard work and soul searching. Looking at your own character traits, downfalls, pride, ego and defects that block the flow of God's power was humbling and difficult at times. The hardest bit being probably repentance and forgiveness. Seeing yourself from God's perspective shone a new light into the situations we were dealing with. Being honest and open was key to me moving forward. I was able to share things I had never told anyone before and pray about some of the most uncomfortable areas of my life. I felt a peace and an ability to share personal things without feeling coaxed into sharing, and without any feeling of judgement or ridicule. I have never sensed this before.

God was good and led us through the steps of the course, which were contained in the program but, in a way, it had nothing to do with the program, if that makes sense? It was all about God, and letting Him in, allowing Him to take control and lead you rather than you thinking you knew better!

Three months into the course I caught Covid 19, despite having had my first jab. Luckily, we had a recent loft bedroom built and I was able to fully isolate away from my family. It was during this time of isolation that God spoke to me in many ways, like I had never experienced or heard before.

Instead of watching television, I watched Christian video clips based on truth and scripture. I watched with new eyes and listened with new ears. Something switched on for me, like a lightbulb. Scriptural truths made sense and slipped into place. Revelation was a daily occurrence. I read more scripture, recognized God's awesomeness, and felt a peace I had never felt before.

God used my weakness to trust and rely on Him completely. During this time, I wasn't worried; God provided food for us via church members, and He kept my son and husband safe. It seems a strange thing to say but I was glad I had Covid, as I may never have been helpless and desperate enough to truly let go and do the suggested work in the course. It also seemed to give me the time to truly *seek*.

Things went from strength to strength from then on. I completed the course and have been accepted back into membership. I've been able to meet up in church again and celebrate my new relationship with God, Jesus and the Holy Spirit in a new and exciting way. I feel like I have had a major breakthrough in my relationships with God and people I have asked forgiveness from, as I have been able to forgive myself as well.

Once we get rid of the clutter and rubbish of our past and open up honestly to God and let Him do the work in you, then amazing things happen. It's the truth!

The New You:
Keeping What You Have

I have been told many times that if I want to keep what I have, I need to give it away. Jesus said to His disciples:

Heal the sick, cleanse the lepers, raise the dead, cast out devils: freely ye have received, freely give.

Matthew 10:8

So, I obey, and do so out of love. However, if I am completely honest I find it is gratitude that motivates me more than anything else. You have heard from my story just how defeated and desperate I'd become. Finally, I'd realized that it was *impossible* for me to create a real relationship with God, and when I told God I was defeated, He orchestrated the various elements (including this Program), which ultimately opened my eyes to the fact that He was there all the time – with me, in me, and I in Him. I quite literally found myself in this real and intimate relationship with Him, as if it had always been this way, it is incredible. I followed the Program and thereby set a solid foundation, while also establishing a genuine relationship with God for the first time in my life. This is an indescribable event, and I feel nothing other than gratitude to God for this. How can

I thank God enough? I simply cannot. The best way to show my gratitude is to pass it on and try to help someone else who might want it and is willing to take the time to listen.

Through the process, I found that the group I attended was one of the important factors. I thank all those guys (and still thank the people in my groups today) who were there for me and who allowed God to work through them to aid me in certain important aspects of my journey. I was not one who liked groups particularly, and in fact I did not like much help from anyone on anything. This was one of my main problems; I thought that I could sort things out myself. I now know that things are actually quite the opposite, and that there are very few things I can sort out on my own. Any ability or opportunity or success I may achieve are all God-given and God-sent, therefore all glory *has* to go to Him. I am just very grateful that He opened my eyes to this and, thereafter, I took to my groups like a duck to water. These people were *real,* with no airs and graces about them. I got hugged solidly (never was a "Huggy" guy) and did not feel awkward because it was genuine. Never before in my life had I come across a bunch of people who were so happy to see me and yet expected nothing from me in return; they just wanted to help. I cannot explain how odd and appealing that felt all at the same time. It was a place I wanted to be, and these people had what I wanted. I too got in on the hugging thing. I used to hug the people and tell them I loved them because, quite simply, I did. This was so out of my character, but when you feel the love God has placed in others, it is hard not to join in and pass it on.

We are meant to meet together. No man is an island, and God made it this way.

Not forsaking the assembling of ourselves together, as the manner of some is; but exhorting one another: and so much the more, as ye see the day approaching.

Hebrews 10:25

What God is saying in this verse is that we should encourage and urge one another on. I think it is natural to run out of steam at times – to feel down and lethargic, and this type of encouragement and support is just what we need.

In summary, there are three reasons why a group like this is important:

- You can learn from others.

- You can help and show others the path to a deeper relationship with God.

- You can both support and be supported by others.

If you are just two people, you can start a group (a group can be anything: home/cell group, Bible study, support group, etc.). If we return to the scriptures, we find confirmation of this principle too:

For where two or three are gathered together in my name, there am I in the midst of them.

Matthew 18:20

So, at a meeting of two the main member, our God, is present automatically. I started my first group with just the person I was mentoring and myself. We worked through the steps, shared struggles, read from the Word, and prayed for one another and others. Eventually, the group grew and got to about twenty, which is when we started a second group at a shelter. It is amazing what God will do if we let Him. Wayne and I sat many a night on our own in the beginning, but it did not matter as we were getting stronger and spending time with God.

Failure or success in terms of numbers has little to do with us and all to do with God. We must just be faithful in carrying the message and willing to share with anyone who wants to listen. Our human nature gets despondent if there are not many people attending, and equally it is our human nature that wants to take accolades if the place is packed out. Both are wrong.

If you start a group meeting, I suggest you do so at your church. Tell them that you will be fully self-supporting but would like to fall under the church's umbrella of ministries.

The structure and format of a meeting can follow these guidelines, or you can follow your own, just as you feel led:

1) The Prayer

   I would suggest opening the meeting with the Lord's Prayer, you could all say it out loud together. You can of course use your own prayers if you like.

2) The Body of the Meeting

   You could try one of three options I suggest, or you might prefer a different approach altogether.

   a. *Going through this book together.* This is the format I recommend. Start right from the beginning, in the introduction, because there is a lot there that will help in preparing for the rest of the book. I feel the meeting should be as close to one hour as possible, and normally take place once a week. Pick someone to read and ask them to stop reading after about 20 minutes or so.

You can then open the meeting for shares and discussion. This time is very important for this kind of meeting as my writing is only an opinion, and every situation and experience is slightly different. Those who can relate to a scenario can share their similar experience, or perhaps a different experience related to that scenario. It is a good time to learn, share and grow. There are no hard and fast rules on any of this, so please do not feel restricted to these formats. If you have other ideas and feel led by the Holy Spirit, by all means implement them. Always remember, though, that this is a Christian group, and always respect the church where you have your meetings.

b. *Sharing meeting.* This I would recommend to a group that has gone through the book and have all completed the Program in it. Everybody gets to share whatever they would like. I find it better to wait until all have shared and then open the meeting to anyone to share their experience on an issue which might be encouraging to another. It is important not to interrupt or criticize another who is sharing.

c. *Scripture reading and topic discussion.* This can be done in any way you would like, and normally it takes on the feel of a Bible study. Someone appointed the week before might bring a topic to the next meeting, along with a few scriptures on that topic. They would share some of their understanding of the topic and read the Bible verses that he or she has selected as relevant. After this you can open the meeting for anyone to share.

3) Prayer

Prayer is an important part of our lives, as this is our direct communication with God. Some meetings can be given over mostly or entirely to prayer. You could pray for circumstances in one another's lives, other people, family, or whatever you want. I believe it is important to thank God for all the blessings in your life, as this shows gratitude for what God has given you and what He has done for you. Prayer is vital and should never be left out of anything we do, that is why we say a prayer together in the beginning, and one at the end to close.

4) Closing

Once the hour is up, I suggest you close with the serenity prayer said aloud together.

"God, grant me the serenity to accept the things I cannot change, courage to change the things I can, and the wisdom to know the difference. In Jesus' name. Amen."

I wish you all the best with your group. You will find yourself really growing as a person. Remember not to have any expectations of the group. Leave the results to God and focus on growing in your relationship with Him.

This might be a good time to speak to you about the benefit of a mentor and what it means to me. A mentor or sponsor can be like a friend, confidant, sounding board, advisor, helper or guide. This is why in my life, and still today, I have a few mentors. There are some who swear by only one sponsor, and that works for them. This is the beauty of the Program, that you can do what works for you as you allow God to guide you. I believe there are incredible benefits to having a mentor, someone to talk to about honest "stuff".

As iron sharpens iron, So one man sharpens [and influences] another [through discussion].

Proverbs 27:17 [AMP]

I believe that my walk with the Lord is immensely enriched by the fact that I have mentors in my life. When I was still living on the Kwa-Zulu Natal South Coast, I had a friend like this who lived just outside of Port Shepstone. He stayed on a sugar cane farm and I would drive up there three times a week and we'd walk in the cane for an hour or two. He was also a recovering alcoholic but had a firm grip on the spiritual aspect of the Program. We would talk non-stop about our days, our hang-ups, our relationships, our victories, and pretty much everything we could. We offered each other moral support and gave each other words of encouragement. This was one of the most supportive relationships I had. There were one or two things that he would not share with me and when I probed, he became very offish. I kept my distance and soon afterwards my wife and I moved to another city.

Another thing I did was join a men's group on a Friday morning before work. We met in a hotel lobby and drank coffee and shared. I am sure you can find something like this in your area. The people don't need to know your situation, but remember that you have many affairs that you need encouragement and support in. The guys in my group do know about my life story, and I am able to make suggestions and help them understand what various people in their lives are going through that may be afflicted with similar issues. How ever you go about it, I understand that it's not easy dealing with people sometimes. But as the Word of God says, we are not meant to be recluses; we are to help others and grow in our relationships. If you find it really tough, just remain willing and it will come. We need to continue to remind ourselves that it is God who is the source of our power, and He will give us the strength to be obedient.

Epilogue

Trust in the LORD with all thine heart; and lean not unto thine own understanding. In all thy ways acknowledge him, and he shall direct thy paths.   Proverbs 3:5-6

This has become one of the most profound pieces of scriptural instruction for Christian living in my life today. During the course of my life, through many years of trial and error, I have finally concluded that it is impossible for me to fully obey this scripture on my own. I fully understand it and the promises it offers, and I wholeheartedly believe that if I get it right, I will be acting in God's perfect will at all times. To me, there is nothing more to Christianity than these two verses. It is saying that we are to trust and obey, nothing more than that. We are required to trust God without any wavering or doubt whatsoever. Then we are to obey what He is saying, which firstly is not to rely on the way we understand things – we're to trust God even when it seems totally ludicrous.

Secondly, we're to acknowledge God in everything, and for me this means to say that however, wherever, and whatever is going on in my life (good or bad), I am to believe that I am totally in God's will, and I am exactly where I'm supposed to be at that precise moment. Once I became His child through salvation in Jesus, this is the truth and it is only deception (mainly from the devil) that prevents me fully believing this, which leads to me subconsciously distancing myself from God.

This feeling of conscious separation from God is what Charles Chamberlain refers to as ego at the Pala Mesa retreat in 1975, and which I closely affiliate to pride and self. As I have described in the book, this is what I believe to be our main hinderance to a full life, and a real and truly intimate relationship with God. The big issue in ridding oneself of pride/ego/self, is that it is impossible for us to see it in ourselves, and so how does one rid oneself of something we don't truly believe we have? God helps us with this through the medium of pain and discomfort, I believe, and if we are not in true relationship with Him, we will be feeling this pain and discomfort. It is then just a question of whether this pain and discomfort is sufficient for us to want to do just about anything to be rid of these feelings.

This is where the solution comes in. I believe that because we have spent so many years of our lives trying to rid ourselves of these feelings of pain and discomfort by trying all the wrong solutions and ways, we have built up some deep-seated character defects. The trouble with the true solution, is that it is the direct opposite to the problem we have, which is the same problem we don't believe we have. Pride/self/ego is the problem, and humility is the solution. God says in James 4:10 that if we do humble ourselves, He will lift us up.

The solution, which is contained in this Program of 12 steps, is a process by which we are able to attain a certain level of unconscious humility, which ultimately allows God to complete the work in us, and He is then able to give us the ability though the power of the Holy Spirit to "trust Him with all our hearts", to "be perfect as He is perfect" and to "love Him with all our heart, soul, strength and mind; and our neighbour as ourselves". I believe we will then be at the point where we are consciously aware of His presence in our lives, and where we have a total belief that He is directing our lives at all times.

It is when this happens that we will be able to live peacefully, joyfully and comfortably with ourselves, firmly grounded in the understanding and sense that we are in close and intimate relation to God, and that truly nothing can separate us from His love. This is my fervent prayer and hope for all.